SO-ASG-387

Cambodian Culture since 1975

Asia East by South

A series published under the auspices of
the Southeast Asia Program, Cornell University

Cambodian Culture since 1975: Homeland and Exile,
edited by May M. Ebihara, Carol A. Mortland, and
Judy Ledgerwood

Also in the series

Southeast Asia in the Early Modern Era: Trade, Power, and Belief
edited by Anthony Reid

*Opium to Java: Revenue Farming and Chinese Enterprise in
Colonial Indonesia, 1860–1910*
by James R. Rush

An Age in Motion: Popular Radicalism in Java, 1912–1926
by Takashi Shiraishi

*Opium and Empire: Chinese Society in Colonial Singapore,
1800–1910*
by Carl A. Trocki

Cambodian Culture since 1975

HOMELAND AND EXILE

EDITED BY

MAY M. EBIHARA

CAROL A. MORTLAND

JUDY LEDGERWOOD

Cornell University Press

ITHACA AND LONDON

First published 1994 by Cornell University Press.

Printed in the United States of America

⊗The paper in this book meets the minimum requirements of the
American National Standard for Information Sciences—Permanence
of Paper for Printed Library Materials, ANSI Z39.48-1984.

Library of Congress Cataloging-in-Publication Data

Cambodian culture since 1975 : homeland and exile / edited by May M.
  Ebihara, Carol A. Mortland, and Judy Ledgerwood.
    p. cm. — (Asia, east by south)
  Includes bibliographical references and index.
  ISBN 0-8014-2967-6 (cloth : alk. paper) ISBN 0-8014-8173-2 (paper : alk. paper)
    1. Cambodia—Politics and government—1975– 2. Cambodia—
Intellectual life. 3. Khmers—Foreign countries. I. Ebihara,
May. II. Mortland, Carol A. (Carol Anne), 1945– .
III. Ledgerwood, Judy, 1959– . IV. Series.
DS554.8.C359   1994
959.604—dc20
                                                        93-43741

To the Khmer

Contents

Acknowledgments

We thank David Chandler for reading earlier drafts of these essays and providing comments, and for kindly consenting to write a preface. We are grateful also to Audrey Kahin and Dolina Millar of Southeast Asia Program Publications at Cornell University for their assistance. Our thanks as well to Kathleen Kearns, Una Moneypenny, and Joanne Hindman of Cornell University Press and to Marilyn Sale, our copyeditor.

M. M. E.
C. A. M.
J. L.

Preface

The political typhoon that swept through Cambodia in the civil war and revolution of the 1970s left perhaps two million of its inhabitants dead and a half million more scattered into exile in foreign countries. Over the next ten years or so, Cambodians at home and in exile set about reconstructing and redefining their culture in many different ways. Only a few, particularly those who had left the country before it was "liberated" in 1975, were able to suggest that nothing significant had happened to Cambodian culture in the 1970s or the years that followed. The millions of Cambodians who survived Democratic Kampuchea, led by the man many of them refer to nowadays as "the contemptible Pot" (Khmer: *a-Pot*), however, knew that as the civil war and later the revolution of the 1970s swept among them, almost (but not quite) out of control, dramatic changes were taking place in social arrangements, values, and perceptions of Cambodia. Some of these changes were ephemeral; others, from the perspective of the 1990s, seem to be more permanent.

The essays collected in this book testify to several aspects of cultural persistence and change. Ironically, like the physical and psychic destruction that characterized the 1970s, the revival, or more properly the birth, of twentieth-century Cambodian cultural studies, exemplified by this book, was a product of those nightmarish years.

Before the 1970s, very few people in academic life were engaged in writing about modern Cambodia; fewer still used Khmer-language sources or information based on field research in the country. May Ebihara, one of the editors of this volume, Milada Kalab, and I were players in a very small band. It was nice, I suppose, to feel like colonial residents presiding over what was then an exotic, almost unnoticed corner of the world; unfortunately, what we wrote received little feedback and was often overshadowed by scholarship that dealt with other countries.

Interest in Cambodia quickened in the United States in the final years of the Vietnam War and particularly after 1975, but with rare exceptions those who wrote about it were journalists or academics who dealt primarily with politics. Linguistically, they approached Cambodia at arms' length. By and large, these writers had no intention of devoting their careers to Cambodia or to studying its culture.

Most of the men and women whose essays appear in this book belong to an even younger generation. Several—including Judy Ledgerwood and Carol Mortland—were drawn toward Cambodian studies by their work with Khmer refugees on the Thai border or in the United States. Two, Khing Hoc Dy and Sam-Ang Sam, are refugees themselves. Most of the non-Khmer learned Cambodian, abandoning the arms'-length approach favored by many earlier writers. In my view, the essays display an extraordinary openness and sensitivity to Cambodian culture, in a broad sense of that term. Those written by non-Khmer are neither orientalist nor condescending. I believe that the essays will also provoke comparisons with other cultures. Reading them in draft and in final form, I was delighted, instructed, and impressed.

The book had its genesis in a panel convened at the Association for Asian Studies annual meeting in Washington, D.C., in April 1989. The session drew an overflow audience in a large room. For "Cambodian hands" like Ebihara and myself, it was thrilling to see a panel dealing with Cambodia at the Association for Asian Studies, where, as far as I'm aware, no panels had ever singled out the country before. This quickening of attention was due in part to the tragedy of the 1970s—the "killing fields"—and in part to Cambodia's intrinsic interest. This volume owes a great deal, however, to Ebihara and Ledgerwood, who organized the panel, and to the dedication and abilities of a generation of younger scholars, including those who gave papers at the meeting. In revised form, four of these papers (by Sam, Karen Fisher-Nguyen, John Marcucci, and Ledgerwood) appear in the pages that follow. The essays by Khing Hoc Dy, William Lobban, Milada Kalab, John Marston, Frank Smith, and Mortland were prepared specifically for this volume.

I feel sure that *Cambodian Culture* will be the first of many volumes—some, I hope, to be written by its contributors—to explore contemporary Cambodian culture in depth. In the meantime, for newcomers and old hands, it offers an engrossing introduction to that variegated, ancient, and beautiful terrain.

DAVID P. CHANDLER

Melbourne

Note on Transliteration:
Franco-Khmer Transcription
System of Franklin E. Huffman

Transcriptions in this book follow the Franco-Khmer transcription system developed by Franklin E. Huffman in 1983.

Consonants		Transcription	Vowels	Transcription	
1st	2d			1st	2d
ក	គ	k	_ _	â	o
ខ	ឃ	kh	_ ͘	ắ	ŭa
	ង	ng	-ា-	a	ea
គ	ឈ	ch	-ា͘-	ă	ŏa/ĕa[b]
ឃ	ឈ	chh/ch[a]	ិ	ĕ	ĭ
	ញ	nh	ី	ey	i
ដ	ណ	d	ឹ	ŏe	ĕu
ឋ, ឍ	ឍ	th	ឺ	oeu	eu
ណ		n	ុ	ŏ	ŭ
ត	ទ	t	ូ	au	ou
ថ	ធ	th		uo	uo
	ន	n	ួ	aoe	oe
		b	ើ	eua	eua
ប	ព	p	ឿ	ie	ie
ុ	ភ	ph	េ	e	é
	ម	m	ែ	ae	ĕ
ប	យ	y	ៃ	ai	ei
	រ	r	ោ	ao	ŏ
	ល	l	ៅ	av	ŏv
	វ	v	ុំ	ŏm	ŭm
ស		s	ាំ	ắm	ŭm

Consonants		Transcription	Vowels	Transcription	
1st	2d			1st	2d
ʊ		h	-ໍ	ăm	ŏam
ຢ		l	-ិង	ăng	ĕang
ម		Ø/ʳᶜ	-ៈ	ăh	ĕah

[a]When followed by another consonant, as in *chnăm* [year].
[b]Before a velar final, as in *nĕak* [person].
[c]When subscript to another consonant, as in *s'at* [clean].

Although this system is similar to that used in many French-language works on Cambodia, additional diacritics act to distinguish all of the various vowel sounds. The system is used as printed above, with the following modifications:

1. No unpronounced finals are written.
2. Final ʊ is written *p*.

Cambodian Culture since 1975

CHAPTER ONE

Introduction

Judy Ledgerwood, May M. Ebihara, and Carol A. Mortland

The tragedy of Cambodia has not yet run its course, nor will it for generations. Millions have died, a culture has vanished.
—Yathay Pin, 1987

Kampuchea was reduced to ashes. The whole Kampuchean people became slaves and convicts under death sentence. The whole social and material infrastructure were destroyed. In no time at all, everything that was built by the Kampuchean people during the last thousand years was torn to pieces.
—*Kampuchea Today,* 1988

We had no more monks and no religious services. We had no more family obligations. Children left their parents to die, wives abandoned their husbands and the strongest kept moving. The Khmer Rouge had taken away everything that held our culture together, and this was the result: a parade of the selfish and the dying. Society was falling apart.
—Ngor Haing, 1987

The perception among Khmer that their culture has been lost, or is being lost, is pervasive. The destruction from years of warfare, the horrendous losses during the years of Democratic Kampuchea (1975–1979), followed by the presence of their traditional enemies, the Vietnamese, and, for hundreds of thousands of Khmer, the new realities of living beyond the borders of their country in camps and in third countries, all raise the anxiety that the Khmer as a people will cease to exist.

This fear is found not only among Khmer refugees in Long Beach, Boston, or Paris but among Khmer in Cambodia as well. When May Ebihara returned to Cambodia to restudy a village where she had done her dissertation research thirty years before, she met with the then minister of information and culture, Chheng Phon. He told her pointedly that she would not find Khmer culture in that village today, that the Khmer Rouge had destroyed the system of social relations which had bound people together. People, he asserted, did not help one another anymore, and the family was no longer bound by the old system of obligations. The Khmer Rouge had "atomized" Khmer society, broken it down into parts that had still not been reconstituted. The statements seemed amazing coming from a man whom many have credited with the restoration of Khmer "culture" through his work on the reestablishment of Khmer music and dance (see also Blumenthal 1989).

Khmer culture has at least partially disappeared. Because of the tremendous loss of lives during the war years and the Democratic Kampuchea period, many skills known only to certain individuals are lost. As Sam-Ang Sam points out in his chapter, "Performing arts do not die, but performers do." Not only dancers, but monks who knew how to chant certain religious texts properly, craftsmen who knew how to construct distinct kinds of ox carts, and women who knew how to weave specific designs perished with their knowledge.

Much of the written documentation on Khmer culture was similarly lost. As a result of the deliberate destruction of texts by the Khmer Rouge, combined with loss from neglect and the effects of the elements, less than half of the Khmer-language materials from before 1975 exist today. For example, the National Library in Phnom Penh has only three hundred unduplicated titles in Khmer, and much of the work of the Commission of Mores and Customs [Commission des Moeurs et Coutumes du Cambodge] has been lost. While the old Buddhist Institute library used to house more than sixteen hundred palm-leaf manuscripts, in Phnom Penh today there are less than eight hundred manuscripts left at four sites (Ledgerwood 1990a).

The loss of cultural artifacts, such as musical instruments, masks for the dance, and Buddhist images, was also tragically high. P. Dyphon writes: "Between 1975 and 1979 the holocaust of Pol Pot and the Khmer Rouge destroyed not only between 2 and 3 million lives, but uncountable artifacts bearing witness to Cambodian culture and civilization. I can give examples of such destruction that I myself witnessed: the decapitation of the large statues of Buddha and the crushing into dust of the smaller ones; the burning of the handsome ceremonial costumes used in dance and weddings; and the confiscation of our personal jewelry" (1988:5). The loss of works of art continues today with the ongoing instability in the country. Archaeological sites fall under the control of different armed groups, and works of Khmer art appear mysteriously on the world's art markets.

In another realm, during the Democratic Kampuchea period the effort to standardize agriculture had the result that many distinct strains of rice were lost as farmers were supplied with only one kind of seed. The International Rice Research Institute is now reintroducing Khmer strains of rice which had been stored outside the country during this period. Many disastrous Democratic Kampuchean irrigation projects not only did not work, but in many areas permanently changed water flow patterns so that farmers returning to their home regions could no longer use their past knowledge to predict and control water movement.

Besides the loss of people, knowledge, and things, there is also the sense of a loss of order in Khmer culture, as Chheng Phon's comments above reflect. The changes in Khmer society during the years of Khmer Rouge rule are sometimes interpreted by Khmer to have been the end of a Buddhist era, the extinction of the world as they knew it (see Smith 1989). New social relations in countries of resettlement are based on cultural models Khmer refugees bring with them from their home country, but take variant forms because of different circumstances (see Mortland and Ledgerwood 1987 and Ledgerwood 1990c on patron-client relationships; Ledgerwood 1990b on gender relationships). Social ties among the hundreds of thousands of Khmer who lived in camps along the Thai-Khmer border are similarly modified (see Reynell 1989; French 1990). Although changes within Cambodia have yet to be studied in depth, certain facts suggest that new patterns of social relations have emerged. For example, demographic shifts due to twenty years of warfare have resulted in an adult population that is in some areas up to 70 percent female (Boua 1981, 1982). This shift has brought about changes in marriage and residence patterns, as well as in the role of women in the workplace (Sonnois 1990; UNICEF 1990; Ledgerwood 1992).

It is not only Khmer who conceive of Khmer culture as having been lost. This notion is common among refugee workers and other westerners who have had contact with Khmer abroad. For example, one scholar suggests, "It would appear that much of the integral national culture, as well as diverse regional folk cultural tradition, of pre-war Cambodia has been lost forever—sundered and strewn about the countryside in the devastation of a people, the dismantling of a culture, and the emasculation of a nation-state with few parallels in contemporary history" (Crystal 1988:13).

This perception of prerevolutionary Khmer culture as having been lost or altered has led to efforts by both Khmer and non-Khmer to save what remains. The Social Science Research Council's Indochina Studies Program was based in part on the idea of conducting a sort of cultural archaeology or salvage ethnography. The cultures of Indochina were studied through the use of Khmer, Lao, and Vietnamese in the United States as sources of information about their homelands. Three of the contributors to this volume (Ledgerwood, Marston, and Sam) conducted their research with grants from this program.

An effort to preserve what remains of Khmer writing and written documentation on Khmer culture led Cornell University Libraries, with funding from the Henry Luce Foundation and the Christopher Reynolds Foundation, to undertake a project in which surviving Khmer documents are saved through microfilming: one copy stays in Phnom Penh and other copies are sent to the United States. Cornell has also microfilmed its Khmer-language holdings and western works on Cambodia and sent them back to the country. Judy Ledgerwood was involved in this project for several years.

Various Cambodian-American organizations have sprung up around the United States with the goal of preserving Khmer culture. The Khmer Studies Institute in Newington, Connecticut, for example, has undertaken a publication series to "preserve and foster the Khmer culture, customs and values" (Ngy 1987:1).

The image of the Khmer as "survivors" and as "victims" also holds a certain fascination for many westerners. Khmer are viewed as remnants of the killing fields, and our interest is held by the sheer power of their story. This interest can lead people, as Michael Vickery (1984) points out, to believe that everything was uniformly horrific, although the situation actually varied greatly throughout the country and over time. The image can motivate authors to use the Khmer example to ponder broader problems in the world (Sheehy 1986; Fawcett 1988). We want to know Khmers' stories for the meaning that they might hold for our own lives. This is one point at which the general view of the Khmer held by the westerner begins to overlap with the questions Khmer ask about their own society and with the questions that are standard fare in anthropology.

The View from an Anthropological Perspective

Concepts of "Cambodian culture" and "Khmer tradition" are cultural constructions or labels placed on certain phenomena. Contemporary anthropology has questioned the very notion of "a culture" as a bounded entity with certain essentialist and static "traditions" (e.g., Wolf 1982). The Khmer, of course, have experienced centuries of sociocultural transformations, and what is considered to be "traditional" may really be historically recent "inventions of tradition" (Hobsbawm and Ranger 1983). The repertoires of Cambodian dance troupes, for instance, include "folk dances" that were actually choreographed during the 1960s and early 1970s (Toni Shapiro, personal communication).

Nonetheless, both western scholars and indigenous Khmer sometimes conceive of certain Khmer cultural features as having persisted from early historical periods, or they may take Cambodia of the 1950s–60s as representing "traditional" Khmer society and culture that were altered in diverse ways during and after Democratic Kampuchea. Indeed, there are historical antecedents for various aspects of modern Cambodian life (see, for example, Chandler 1983, 1991; Thion 1983); and one may find it heuristically useful or even necessary to use prerevolutionary Cambodia as a "base line" to discuss post-1970s changes in Khmer existence both in the homeland and elsewhere. At the same time, however, one must remember that the term "Cambodian culture" is an intellectual construct and that "Khmer traditions" (as so defined by both scholars and native Khmer) have long undergone transformations wrought by both endogenous and exogenous forces.

Within anthropology since the end of World War II, there has been a steady shift in emphasis from studying "structure" to studying "process." While "repetition and reproduction" are also processes, it is change that has captured the attention of anthropologists (Moore 1986:321). In general, change is assumed to be a constant, and the causes, consequences, and patterns of change become the focus of study.

Sally Falk Moore writes that in this search to uncover "the social logic of transformations," studies have tended to follow one of two models: a "two-system model" or an "individual-centered model" (1986:321). The former understands change by analyzing the contact between two groups, the "traditional" and the "modern," the "capitalist" and "precapitalist," the "developed" and the "developing," or other such categorizations. The works in this group include some Marxist studies, works on the effects of neo-colonialism, and studies of the impact of a "global economy." As the terminology implies, these models are sometimes linked to evolutionary assumptions that societies are moving from one form to another.

In the second type of model, "transformation emerges from the way people constitute a changing social reality in the course of practice or, in another version, interaction, or in making individual choices that cumulatively have large-scale effects" (Moore 1986: 322). This type of model has the advantage of hovering close to the data, which is observable on a local level. After attacking both models for various reasons, Moore argues that what are needed are more studies that integrate small- and large-scale processes, while also being located within the dimension of a particular time.

Studies of refugees in the United States and other western countries have tended to follow these dual theoretical perspectives. In these studies, the two-system model is called "assimilation" or "acculturation." Khmer are moving from one state to another, and the second state, that of being "an American" or "an Australian," is assumed. Some works even presume to measure the progress toward this inevitable conclusion.

Other works focus on the daily life of Khmer abroad and their interaction with the larger host society. In general, these discuss the range of options now available in the new context and the process whereby individuals make choices from within this range of possibilities. The best of these works start from the position that for first-generation refugees abroad, the perspectives from which they will view things and the meanings they will ascribe in a given situation are based primarily in the culture of the motherland (see Van Esterik 1980; Haines 1985; Mortland and Ledgerwood 1987; Donnelly 1989). As Khmer try to act according to Khmer standards in the new context, they must also adapt to living in a new environment. But they need not admit that modification has occurred. Nancy D. Donnelly notes that refugees overlook and accept differences and substitutions in the ways they can practice their traditions in the new land (1989).

This work attempts to combine two perspectives: to provide some of the larger context by viewing the Khmer as people affected by national and international events, and at the same time to focus on the level of individuals and the process whereby they make decisions. Khmer culture is changing, yet Khmer speak of it as unchanging, indeed unchangeable. Their conception has an inherent contradiction: on the one hand, they view Khmer culture as dying or as having died; on the other hand, their fear of losing their culture leads them to the conviction that nothing should be changed.

Khmer as Anthropologists

Although Khmer speak as though the only alternatives are the end of the existence of Khmer culture or retaining this culture, what Khmer are in fact doing, in their country and abroad, is what human beings usually do. They are using key symbols and cultural scenarios restated as "tradition" to adapt to new situations. Although such "reinvention of tradition" (see Hobsbawm and Ranger 1983) is common, the experiences of the Khmer in the last twenty years give rise to particular reasons why this type of activity has become central to their sense of who they are as a people. The very thought that the events of the Democratic Kampuchea years constituted the end of a Buddhist era (*kalpa*) brings the Khmer to reexamine basic cultural concepts (see Smith 1989). In general, they have a heightened awareness of "culture" and the need to examine what were previous givens.

The question of how Khmer could inflict such suffering on fellow Khmer is of particular importance. The stated goal of the Sociology Institute in Phnom Penh was to find, within the attributes that constitute the Khmer character, the flaws that led to the Khmer Rouge years (Vandy Kaon 1981).[1] This need to explain how overwhelming atrocities can occur is shared by other survivors. Barbara Myerhoff (1978) writes about elderly Jewish holocaust survivors in America:

> It was not merely these elders' proximity to their own deaths that so enlivened them—rather it was due to their survival of loved ones, the guilt and responsibility this gendered, and the subsequent necessity for understanding what had brought about the destruction of their people and their natal world. These were what turned them so strongly toward the symbolic life.(25)

> "It can't happen to me," comforts on-lookers but not survivors themselves. They know by what slender threads their lives are distinguished from those who died; they do not see in themselves soothing virtues or special merits that make their survival inevitable or right. They know how easily it could have happened to them; to these people complacency is forever lost. (24)

Survivors, Myerhoff writes, need to recreate an orderly universe. They need both to understand what it is that has happened to them and to have a sense that they now live in a structured, ordered world. They have a "heightened desire for interpretation, for finding the comprehensible elements in their experience" (25).

For Khmer refugees abroad, the issue of the importance of symbols and their interpretations have been discussed from a slightly different angle by two of the authors in this book. Mortland (1987), building on the work of Margie Nowak (1984), discusses refugees as liminal persona. Lederwood (1990b) continues this discussion and applies the concept generally to Khmer in the camps and to Khmer resettled in the United States. Essentially, Nowak argues that during the liminal period and symbol "accumulates connotations." In the extended period of liminality which is refugee life, a dual process occurs: "The extensions of meaning suggested by the evolving metaphor add further import to the original signification." Thus the term "gains in ambiguity as it becomes applied more innovatively to newer broader referents" (1984:162). Images such as Angkor Wat or the dancing aspara [âbsâra] are used in new contexts with new meanings, while at the same time retaining the importance attached to their original identification as "truly Khmer." In the face of a threatened loss of their culture, Khmer emphasize certain cultural symbols as the embodiment of "Khmerness."

In this book, we discuss Khmer trying to preserve their culture, trying to define what Khmer culture is, and trying to fit their culture within new contexts.

Historical Background

The Khmer first came to historical light as a polity in the latter half of the first millennium A.D. Khmer political power increased until it dominated the region from the ninth to the fifteenth centuries during the Angkor period. This time was characterized by a complex sociopolitical organization observing divine kinship and producing distinctive art and monumental architecture.

The following several centuries saw the decline of the Angkorean empire as it shrank in size to approximately that of present-day Cambodia. As a polity, it continued to be threatened by both neighboring Thailand and Vietnam. France colonized Cambodia in the 1860s, preserving it as an entity. French domination, briefly checked by Japanese occupation during World War II, came increasingly to be challenged by the Khmer (Chandler 1974, 1983).

Cambodia gained formal independence from France in 1954. The name of the newly autonomous nation, formally called the Kingdom of Cambodia (Royaume du Cambodge), underwent several changes over the following decades. These successive

renamings were not just linguistic whims but reflected serious political, economic, and sociocultural developments and transformations as different governments came to power.

The Khmer were the politically and numerically dominant ethnic group in the Kingdom of Cambodia in the 1950s and 1960s,
comprising some 85–90 percent of the population. They occupied
both the top and lower social strata as aristocrats, government officials, military officers, Buddhist monks, peasants, artisans,
skilled and unskilled laborers. During this period, the ranks of
business people, white-collar workers, and professionals were
filled largely (although not exclusively) by Chinese and Vietnamese, although each group constituted approximately only 5 percent
of the total population. Intermarriage between Chinese and Khmer
was not uncommon, but Sino-Khmer were not a distinct ethnic
group and were generally socialized culturally as either Khmer or
Chinese (Willmott 1967).

Cambodia has always been agrarian nation with limited indus-
trialization. The majority of the population lived in rural villages
as peasant cultivators of rice, vegetables, and fruit; as artisans producing wares such as cloth or pottery; and as fisherfolk. Most
peasants were small landholders (the national average was about
four acres of land per household), growing crops for family sub-
sistence and, in some cases, for sale. Although rural households
were self-sufficient in many respects, they also engaged in the market exchange of commodities that were part of both national and
international trade networks.

On assuming independence, the government organized itself as
a constitutional monarchy. The king was a figurehead, and effective political power was vested in a prime minister, cabinet, and
legislature. The political scene was overwhelmingly dominated by
Prince Norodom Sihanouk, who abdicated his position as king in
1955 (ceding the throne to his father) to become prime minister.
The respect and support he received from the common people continued to be linked to their concept of royal authority. Sihanouk
has often been characterized as a paradoxical figure, who displayed considerable political savvy but also quixotic and heedless
behavior. For the first twelve years of his rule, Cambodia was relatively stable and peaceful and managed to maintain a neutralist

stance that played the United States, China, and the Soviet bloc against one another.

Toward the end of the 1960s, however, Cambodia's stability was increasingly threatened by both internal and external forces that Sihanouk could not adequately handle. Economic difficulties, endemic corruption, growing alienation between the people and the government, the growth of a militant communist insurgency, and repercussions from the raging conflict in neighboring Vietnam threatened the country's stability.

By 1970, Sihanouk could no longer juggle increasing pressures from participants in the Vietnam War and internal opposition from both the left and the right. He was toppled from power by the National Assembly in the spring of 1970, was replaced by Lon Nol, and the country called itself the Khmer Republic. Political and economic difficulties, caused in part by the Vietnam War and the incompetent governing of Lon Nol, were increased by the growth of the Cambodian communists, whom Sihanouk had dubbed the "Khmer Rouge." From 1970 to 1975, they rapidly extended their control over the country and its population while simultaneously wreaking havoc with Lon Nol's military forces and the country's economy and infrastructure. Fighting between government troops and the Khmer Rouge devastated much of the countryside, as did the United States' "strategic bombing." Although this bombing was undertaken to destroy communist enclaves within Cambodia, it also caused much damage to civilian areas (see Shawcross 1979; Kiernan 1989). By 1975, Phnom Penh was swollen to five times its size by an influx of Khmer fleeing from the countryside, while those remaining in rural areas came increasingly under the rule of the Khmer Rouge.

The Khmer Rouge overcame the American-supported Lon Nol forces and marched into Phnom Penh on April 17, 1975. The small, tight-knit group of Khmer Rouge leaders, most of whom had studied Marxism together in Paris years earlier, envisioned a new society free from the injustice and influence of western, colonialist, imperialist outsiders. The new government, which lasted until 1979, was called Democratic Kampuchea. Over time and throughout the country, the Khmer Rouge began variously to institute revolutionary changes the eventually led to the devastation

of previous ways of life. The new forms of organization and ideology instigated by the Cambodia communist revolutionaries involved three major transformations (see, for example, Kiernan and
Boua 1982; Kiernan 1985; Ebihara 1987, 1993; Ablin and Hood
1987; Chandler, Kiernan, and Boua 1988; Jackson 1989; Chandler 1991).

First, Democratic Kampuchea's strategy for rebuilding Cambodia's economy, which had been badly disrupted by the war, was
collectivization. The goal was to make Cambodia economically
self-sufficient by maximizing agricultural production. The Khmer
Rouge tried to accomplish this by evacuating urban areas and con-
verting the entire population into agricultural laborers organized
into communes made up of work units. These cooperatives owned
land, animals, and equipment in common and, in theory, commu-
nally distributed all resources.

While it has been implied (Vickery 1984, 1987; Twining 1989)
that only city people suffered under Democratic Kampuchea rule
because they could not stand the rigors of rural life, peasants also
suffered (Ebihara 1993; Frieson 1990). In particular, peasants
complain about the reordering of society undertaken by the Khmer
Rouge. They grew rice as before, but in work teams rather than as
family and village groups. Most important, after they had produced the rice under forced-labor conditions, it was taken from
them. Khmer commonly ask the outside researcher as well as one
another, "Where did the rice go?" "I don't understand where the
rice went" (see also Chandler and Kiernan 1983; Ledgerwood
1990b). Previously, the rural Khmer grew food and kept it. During
the Democratic Kampuchean regime, they produced food under
unpleasant conditions, and yet they saw little of the fruits of their
labor. What little food they were given had to be eaten under conditions they also disliked; communal dining was particularly de-
spised. Many deaths resulted from malnutrition or outright
starvation.

Second, the reorganization of Democratic Kampuchea's population into work teams caused disruption of the family unit. As the
cooperative became the principal unit for the organization of labor
tasks and the distribution of the tools and products of labor, the
family was superseded in importance. The Khmer Rouge exercised

power over people as individuals, thereby reducing any threat that the family might represent to their absolute control.

Children were often separated from parents, and adolescents were usually grouped in mobile working units located at some distance from their families. As children were physically separated from parents, parents ceased to have authority over them. Husbands and wives could also be separated from one another. The extended family, and in many cases even the nuclear family as an economic and residential unit, ceased to exist, as did its ability to control, support, and comfort its members.

Third, just as the Democratic Kampuchean leaders undertook to destroy the power and security of the Khmer family in their efforts to create a new society, so they also attacked Cambodian religious beliefs. Cambodian Theravada Buddhism, Islam, and Christianity, the latter practiced by only a few Khmer, were ruthlessly suppressed. Theravada Buddhism had been the state religion of Cambodia, and its importance in prerevolutionary Cambodia can scarcely be overstated. The village temple was the center of village life, and most young men entered the monkhood for a period of time. Under Pol Pot, many temples were destroyed, monks were killed or forced to break their vows (by working or being forced to marry), and ritual activity was forbidden.[2]

In place of religion, tradition, and the family, the Khmer Rouge instituted a political ideology that stressed new values and codes of conduct. The Khmer Rouge demanded strict adherence to their rules, which dealt with everything from work to speech to clothing. Punishment for transgressors was swift and harsh. Although the Democratic Kampuchean reign was brief, Khmer describe it as seemingly endless. Their previous existence was destroyed, and the horrors they experienced went on day after day—as one Khmer woman put it, "over one thousand, three hundred days of hell."

The reign of Khmer Rouge terror resulted in the death of hundreds of thousands of Cambodians; estimates range as high as three million, with most scholars agreeing that Democratic Kampuchea was responsible for the deaths of at least one and a half million of its own people (for varying figures, see Kiernan and Boua 1982; Vickery 1984; Jackson 1989; Kiernan 1990). These deaths resulted not only from direct execution but from beatings, hard labor, malnutrition, debilitation, and illness. The Khmer Rouge directed their destruction not only against ordinary people but against their own cadre and former allies; widespread purges and executions occurred repeatedly.

Democratic Kampuchea's relationship to its former allies, the Vietnamese communists, had always been ambiguous and vacillating. After the Khmer Rouge captured Phnom Penh, Democratic Kampuchea attacked Vietnam along the Vietnam-Kampuchea border. By 1978 armed conflict between the two governments had escalated, and in late 1978 Vietnam invaded Cambodia, allied with former Khmer Rouge cadres who had fled purges and staged a rebellion in the eastern zone of the country (see Chanda 1986). Phnom Penh was captured by the Vietnamese in January 1979. The Khmer Rouge retreated to the west and established guerrilla bases along the Thai-Cambodian border.

The Vietnamese and their Khmer allies quickly set up a new government, the People's Republic of Kampuchea. The new regime was composed of Cambodians, but Vietnamese soldiers bolstered the country's military capacity. The withdrawal of the Vietnamese troops in the fall of 1989 convinced all but some overseas Khmer and the resistance factions that the government was then Khmer and relatively independent from neighboring Vietnam.

In 1979 there were massive movements of Khmer: within the country as they sought to find lost relatives and return to their villages or reach safe shelter, as they were forced to accompany the retreating Khmer Rouge cadre, or as they fled to Thailand in search of food and security (Heder 1980a, 1980b, 1980c, 1981). Fighting between the retreating Khmer Rouge forces and the invading Vietnamese, the migration of Khmer throughout the country, disruption of the agricultural cycle, and a lack of draft animals and seed created famine conditions that were relieved only through international assistance.

Population statistics are one indicator of the tragedy that swept Cambodia. Cambodia's population was estimated at over seven million in 1970 (Migozzi 1973). It has been observed (Cheriyand and FitzGerald 1989) that rather than the 11.5 million than would normally have been expected in 1989 from an annual growth rate of 2.7 percent, Cambodia's 1989 population was only 8.4 million, the difference resulting from the effects of war for over two decades. It is estimated that approximately 60–65 percent of the adult population is female, and nearly half of the population is under fifteen years of age (Cheriyand and FitzGerald 1989; UNICEF 1990).

Throughout the 1980s, Cambodia slowly began a recovery that continues today. People repopulated the cities and towns, villages were rebuilt, families were reunited, and Buddhism was revived. Government and economic institutions were reestablished and the infrastructure slowly reconstructed. This government also initially tried collectivized agriculture, but the *krŏm samâki* (communal work team) system proved both unpopular and unproductive and was slowly abandoned during the 1980s (Kiernan and Boua 1982; Vickery 1986, 1984; Frings 1993). In 1989 the country's name was changed to the State of Cambodia, and a new constitution was written which includes ownership of private property and freedom of religion. (On various aspects of Cambodia's recent history and contemporary life, see Volkman 1990.)

Economic recovery was severely hampered throughout this period by the ongoing civil war. Resistance armies were Prince Sihanouk's National United Front for an Independent, Neutral, Peaceful and Co-operative Cambodia (FUNCINPEC), Son Sann's Khmer People's National Liberation Front (KPLNF), and the Khmer Rouge, the Party of Democratic Kampuchea (PDK). These factions continued their activities on the Thai-Cambodian border and threatened the Phnom Penh administration. An international blockade of Cambodia prevented its participation in significant loan and assistance programs and thus prevented serious development efforts.

Reconstruction efforts by the People's Republic of Kampuchea and relief assistance by nongovernmental organizations within the country, on the one hand, and resettlement from the border to third world countries, on the other, were not resolving the problems resulting from the previous two decades of war in Cambodia. The blockage of international assistance along with the loss of much of the skilled labor force and the traumatization of the population hindered economic development (see Mysliwiec 1988). In addition, hundreds of thousands of Khmer who had fled to neighboring countries did not gain the sanctuary they sought. At least 400,000 returned home from Thailand, Laos, and Vietnam in the 1980s (United States Committee for Refugees 1990).

In 1991 over 16,000 Cambodian refugees remained in Vietnam, and approximately the same number languished in camps in Thailand supervised by the United Nations High Commissioner for Refugees.[3] Approximately 270,000 displaced Khmer were held in other Thai border camps served by the United Nations Border Relief Operation. These displaced Khmer had no opportunity to seek resettlement in third countries and were utilized by the three Cambodian resistance armies for manpower and resources. An additional 50,000 displaced Khmer in villages and military camps on the Thai-Cambodian border lived under the control of the Khmer Rouge and were isolated from international assistance (U.S. Bureau for Refugee Programs 1990; United States Committee for Refugees 1990). Inside Cambodia, there were also approximately 250,000 displaced persons who had fled fighting in the country during 1991.

In October 1991 the four warring factions signed a peace agreement in Paris. Norodom Sihanouk returned to Phnom Penh in November as head of the Supreme National Council, a body with members from all four factions which acted in an advisory capacity until elections were held in 1993.

The United Nations Transitional Authority in Cambodia (UNTAC) deployed over twenty thousand personnel, including fifteen thousand soldiers, to oversee the ceasefire between the factions and to organize and supervise the election process. UNTAC also theoretically monitored the daily operations of five key ministries of the existing administrative structures: defense, interior, finance, foreign affairs and information. It undertook rehabilitation projects and the repatriation of more than 350,000 refugees from the Thai-Cambodia border.

The Khmer Rouge refused to participate in the peace process and did not canton or disarm any of their forces. They actively tried to disrupt the operations of the United Nations forces, and on several occasions attacked UN personnel. The refusal of the Khmer Rouge to participate severely limited UNTAC's ability to force compliance with implementing the agreement by other signatories. The months before the election saw continued human rights abuses, the harassment of opposition political parties and in some cases murder of party workers. The Khmer Rouge also massacred ethnic Vietnamese living in Cambodia.

In spite of these problems, the elections held in May 1993 were a resounding success. More than 90 percent of the registered voters turned out to vote, more than 42 percent of the voters crowding into the polling stations on the first day. Cambodian voters had been inundated with propaganda from the Khmer Rouge saying that anyone who voted was a "traitor to the nation" and would be subject to elimination. They had also been pressured by the State of Cambodia administration to vote for the existing government. The royalist FUNCINPEC party won 45 percent of the vote and formed a coalition government with the Cambodian People's Party (the party of the SOC administration), who won 38 percent. The Buddhist Liberal Democratic Party was 3.8 percent with the remainder split between the other seventeen smaller parties.

Since the election, the constituent assembly has met and written a new constitution. The new government declared itself a monarchy, and Norodom Sihanouk has again been crowned king. The Khmer Rouge remain in the jungle at the time of this writing, although they have had discussions with Sihanouk about joining the new government in some capacity. During clashes with the new government's combined army, it was reported that large numbers of Khmer Rouge troops were deserting.

The United States has dropped its economic embargo against Cambodia, opening the door both for business investment and for Cambodia's participation in international development programs. Western countries as well as Asian neighbors have opened embassies and begun bilateral assistance programs.

The capital city, Phnom Penh, has changed dramatically in the last three years. The tremendous influx of capital has created an improved standard of living for some but not all. The streets are filled with cars and motorcycles. Many new assistance programs have begun, but serious problems have arisen as well. Land speculation during the UNTAC period drove up the price of housing in the city beyond what most Khmer could afford. Shantytowns grew around the perimeter of the city. Corruption was commonplace. Some soldiers, from different factions, shed their uniforms but not their weapons and turned to banditry. A nightclub and prostitution industry boomed overnight to serve the UN soldiers as well as the influx of wealthy Asian businessmen.

Although there is a potential for lasting peace, the situation in Cambodia remains uncertain. Hundreds of thousands of Khmer who are now living as residents in other countries increasingly recognize that the difficulties of resettlement in third countries are not temporary but will endure throughout their lifetimes. Before 1970, few Khmer had traveled or resided abroad, and those who had were familiar primarily with France. A little more than a decade later, Khmer refugees are scattered across the world, having been granted resettlement in nineteen countries. Most went to the United States, which had accepted approximately 150,000 Khmer by 1992. An additional 70,000 Khmer were resettled in other western countries, including France, Australia, Canada, and Spain.

The Refugee Context

This review of Cambodian history and the Khmer Rouge years may help the readers to understand Khmer refugee life in the United States and other countries. But Khmer refugees have endured additional experiences that color their resettlement lives and that they have in common with other refugees. These include the horror of war, flight from their homeland, residence in refugee camps in other countries, a subsequent decision to remain a refugee whatever the costs and not to return to their land of origin, resettlement in still a third country, and an eventual incorporation into the new country, although never to the satisfaction of the refugee or the surrounding community.

There is a way to conceptualize these successive experiences that vividly demonstrates their influence on the people who have endured them. One needs to abandon a view of Khmer refugees as biculturals, people who come from one culture and now live in a second, and exchange it for a perspective that sees war, flight, camp life, and resettlement as a series of distinctive cultural experiences that have far-reaching impact on refugees. "Being Khmer" is a particular and cultural orientation set within a particular context shared only by other Cambodians. An awareness of Khmer culture is not sufficient for an understanding of the varied experiences of Khmer refugees.[4]

The Khmer have survived the horrors of modern warfare. Many experienced the terror of living through B-52 bombing raids, of having friends and relatives killed in fighting as combatants or as bystanders. Thousands had to flee their homes and lands to hide in the cities to escape the carnage. This initial break with normalcy was the beginning for some of twenty years of uncertainty, fear, and powerlessness.

During and after the Democratic Kampuchea years, some Khmer then made the difficult decision to flee their homeland. For a refugee, this involves the perception that one has no option but to leave, that flight from all one has known into the unknown is preferable to life as it has been. In making this choice, people focus on the perceived advantages and disadvantages of staying or going. The decision process centers on the loss that has already occurred and anticipated future loss. Despite the tragedy and loss they have already experienced, people contemplating flight dread the unknown and the additional horrors they suspect will occur. In understanding the choice to escape, we must look at how a refugee views a situation, not at the factual reality, because refugees make this vital determination to flee with little or inaccurate information.

Refugees are willing to enter the unknown because previous security systems have failed and the unfamiliar is preferable to the familiar. Certainly one of the most eloquent descriptions of emotion during flight is that of Yathay Pin, writing of his escape from Cambodia: "I headed west, a dead soul, pushed by my voice. I felt strangely light, freed of hope, freed of fear. I, who had once been so ambitious and so confident, had lost everything. I had been unable to save two of my children, I had abandoned a third, and now I had lost my wife. I had nothing left to lose. What was there to fear? No longer fearing destruction, I was indestructible." (1987:202).

Anyone inclined to underestimate the importance of flight to
Cambodian refugees needs only to listen to them recount their experiences, the essence of which is fear. Their nearly four years under the Khmer Rouge and years of resettlement are summarized in
a few sentences; their few days (at the most, months) of flight are
described at length.

Once they had fled, Khmer refugees shared the experience of
life in refugee camps in Thailand. Here, all political, social, and
economic aspects of life were controlled by others. Certainly
Thailand's hospitality toward Cambodians since 1978 was capri-
cious, variably welcoming and rejecting, offering often dubious
resources and services. Cambodian refugees, if only quietly, frequently judged it a more difficult place to exist than in post–Pol
Pot Cambodia.

This stage of liminality, of being neither what you were nor
what you will become, is characterized primarily for the refugee by
powerlessness. Refugees cannot control the most basic activities of
their lives: procuring food, water, and fuel. They do not know how
long they will be where they are or how to change this situation.
Refugees are exploited by others, even by themselves, in what Al
Santoli calls the "violent limbo in the border camps" (1988:11).

The experience of refugee camp life is shared by others across
the world who have had similar experiences. Some of the anguish
of refugee camp life is reflected in the activities refugees take up
with passion after reaching a settlement site in another country.
The purchase, preparation, and sharing of food, for example, takes
on importance approaching obsession after years of food depriva-
tion and inability to choose what foods to eat.

Khmer refugees, finally, share with other refugees the experience of starting life again in a new place. Resettlement is the po-
larity, the second half, of the bicultural model. Americans trying to
understand Khmer refugees in the United States explain behavior
they do not understand by saying, "That is Cambodian." It may
be, but it has been influenced by the intervening experiences and
by the particularities of the experiences of being newcomers in a
strange environment.

The sense of powerlessness for refugees generally continues in
the new context, particularly for Khmer, because they have expe-

rienced such extreme levels of brutality (Kinzie 1987:347). The legacy of these survivors also includes pain—real, physical pain. Khmer refugees in resettlement countries experience what has been referred to as the "Pol Pot syndrome": "non-specific pains, insomnia, loss of appetite, palpitations and difficulties in breathing" (Swain 1985). In one survey in California, 84 percent of Cambodian households reported a member under a physician's care compared to 45 percent for Vietnamese and 24 percent for Hmong and Lao (Ebihara 1985).

Khmer refugees have an overwhelming compulsion to remember and to recount, to tell the story of their experiences. A young Khmer student says, "I will occasionally lay down and recall my earlier life. It is not that I want to recall such thoughts; it just happens naturally" (Kchao 1989:13). And it is the survivors' burden to tell the story of what happened to others. May Someth writes: "My experiences were no different from those of my family and friends. Any of us could tell the same story. But unlike so many of us, I managed to survive. The revolution forced me to become a liar, a thief, a smuggler, a classical dancer, a refugee and finally a stateless person. And now that I have survived I want to tell the story, exactly as it happened" (1986:18). Khmer refugees experience a combined need to explain to others what has happened to them, and to learn to live as others do in this new place. In this process, there is a shift in emphasis from their own goals, which they may now have to abandon, to a focus on the lives of their children.

Each of these identities, as Cambodians, as survivors of war, as those who have made the decision to flee their country, as residents of refugee camps, and as resettled refugees, has an impact on the choices they make as individuals and on the way that Khmer culture will change in the new world.

The Chapters of This Book

This volume brings together scholars from linguistics, social/cultural anthropology, history, and ethnomusicology to examine continuities and transformations in different spheres of Khmer culture. The contributors include both established scholars and a new generation of Cambodia specialists. They speak Khmer and have had varied experiences and contacts with Khmer, including academic research with Khmer informants, work in refugee camps, social service, teaching, and residence in Cambodia before 1975 and after 1979. The research on which these essays are based was conducted in Cambodia, the United States, France, and in refugee camps in Thailand and the Philippines. Most of the contributors have done fieldwork in several sites.

Our central focus is an exploration of some fundamental values, cultural conceptions, and behaviors in Khmer culture. The essays consider how some features of Khmer culture have persisted despite severe turmoils, while others have been altered or re-created by multiple forces. We are exploring what it is to be Cambodian in a rapidly changing world, how Khmer who are stripped of their customary context for defining what it means to be Cambodian redefine and reidentify themselves, as well as how they utilize traditional forms in new ways and new forms within a traditional framework.

We draw the subsections for this book from several areas that Khmer emphasize as vital to this process of retaining and restating culture: fine arts, Buddhism, language, and fundamental culture concepts. None of the chapters deals with agriculture or daily life in the countryside, partly because most of the research was conducted with Khmer refugees in third countries. But the contents of the volume also reflect the importance of certain realms of culture which are perceived by Khmer themselves as critical to Khmer culture.

In line with the general theme of the book, transformation and persistence, loss and continuity, we have tried to arrange the contributions as contrasts with one another, so that the essays reflect the examinations by both Khmer and scholars of Khmer culture of what Khmer culture is and how it is changing.

The first group of chapters deals with Khmer fine arts; the arts, particularly music and dance, are often taken as the hallmarks of Khmer culture. Like the image of Angkor Wat, they embody what it is to be Khmer. Khing Hoc Dy and Sam-Ang Sam review the current state of Khmer literature and Khmer music respectively, presenting an overview of the last nineteen years both inside and outside Cambodia. Both are critical of the SOC government in Phnom Penh, yet both had an appreciation for the quality of work being done inside the country. Sam points out that it is within Cambodia that the preservation and development of traditional Khmer music will occur.

Lobban's article describes a particular dance performance in 1990 near Phnom Penh. His aim is to document a case in which a specific art form was revived and the circumstances that made this revival possible. In contrast to the overviews, his work provides details of one instance in which an art came alive again, regenerated by surviving performers with minimal resources. That such theater was revived in the countryside and not simply in Phnom Penh attests to its importance among the general populace, both rural and urban.

Like the dance, Buddhism—the subject of the next two chapters—is often associated with the essence of the Khmer spirit. To be Khmer is to be Buddhist, say both Khmer and observers. Kalab and Mortland write about Khmer Buddhism among refugees abroad, in France and in America respectively, but their focuses are quite different. Kalab discusses the institution, the temple [vât] and the organization of monks, and the ways in which these function in a new context. While there are changes—in fact, Kalab notes that it is impossible in the new physical and social circumstances of France to re-create the details of rituals and decorations exactly— the vât is a know entity reconstituted in a new place. Her article provides a sense of how the vât has altered in form but does not challenge the conception of the vât as an institution or Buddhism as a system of beliefs. One might note, too, that the connection between religion and politics is not a new phenomenon. Buddhism and the sângkh (order of monks) in Cambodia, as in other parts of southeast Asia, have engaged in political activities at various historical times and places, especially in urban centers and at elite temples.

Mortland's work, on the other hand, looks specifically at Buddhist conceptions that describe the world and how it operates, and why these no longer provide adequate explanations. Khmer religious concepts become strained, in some cases to the breaking

point, by the need to explain the "inexplicable," that is, the relationship between the Democratic Kampuchean years and lives before and after Pol Pot. If religion is a way of seeing, a prism
through which Khmer view the world around them so that life
is meaningful, what happens when the prism itself is called into
question?

The Khmer language is, of course, another primary key to ideas
of ethnicity; to be Khmer is to speak Khmer. But in looking at
Khmer language, the two essays focus here not just on words and
grammatical structures but on ways of presenting imagery. Fisher-
Nguyen's work on proverbs offers an introduction to Khmer "collective wisdom." The proverbs are important both for the
dominant themes they present and for the sampling they give us of
Khmer style. Fisher-Nguyen's presentation is based largely on
written sources from more stable times, but one important aspect
of Khmer proverbs is that they are commonly stated from memory
and widely used both in Cambodia and Khmer refugees to make
cogent points (see Fisher-Nguyen in this book and Ledgerwood
1990b). Thus, for example, on proverb—"When the hollow gourd
sinks, the clay pot floats"—is nowadays used almost exclusively to
describe the social upheaval in Cambodia during the Khmer Rouge
years. Many Khmer view that period as one in which people previously on the bottom of the social ladder rose to positions of authority, while those formerly on the top sank to the bottom.
Proverbs may have a certain ambiguity (similar to that of the gender symbolism discussed by Ledgerwood in a later section of this
volume) that allows for various interpretations and hence adaptation to present-day life and problems.

Marston focuses on the dramatic changes wrought during the
Democratic Kampuchea years. The Khmer Rouge use of language,
Marston suggests, had consistency, and by examining the metaphors they used we may come to understand more about the con-
sistencies as well as the discontinuities of Khmer revolutionary
language. Metaphor can allow the possibility of taking something
already familiar to refer to something new. Thus there is in the
metaphor an implicit link between past and present.

The two papers complement one another in a way that
reinforces Marston's argument. For example, consider Fisher-

Nguyen's discussion of how images used in proverbs are drawn from the familiar, everyday aspects of rice production and animal husbandry, plants and trees, landscape and household items and how this familiarity enhances the persuasiveness of the proverb. This insight fits clearly, if eerily, with Marston's discussion of how Khmer Rouge language could take something "modest, everyday and homely and use it in a way that it somehow suggests something fearful, overwhelming, and awesome."

The final section examines "traditional" cultural constructs in several critical domains of life—gender, pain, and perceptions of "reality"—as they operate in new contexts. Gender symbolism, Ledgerwood has argued elsewhere (1990b), constitutes a set of social relationships, the preservation of which Khmer consider critical to the retention of Khmer cultural identity. Focusing on a single folk tale and its retellings, she suggests that the nature of gender symbolism allows for a range of acceptable options that are both "traditional" and ambiguous, even contradictory. Thus, a story may be used in completely new situations, playing on this inherent ambiguity to provide "innovative solutions under the rubric of 'tradition.' " Both Marcucci and Smith consider Khmer ways of looking at the world and assumptions about how, in fact, the world actually "is." In Marcucci's discussion of Khmer conceptions of pain and the sharing of pain, he illuminates the articulation between traditional medical practices and Khmer ideas of social relations.

Smith describes refugee Khmer peasants who use the cultural framework from their mother country to interpret media presentations in their new environment. (An interesting comparison could be made between Smith's piece and Lobban's description of the *lkhaon* performance.) Although the three papers in this section may seem very different, they are bound by a common perspective. To understand Khmer refugees in America, we must look to Khmer cultural assumptions: there are particularly Khmer ways of symbolizing gender, experiencing pain, and understanding action videos.

Although Khmer culture is changing in new environments, the fact remains that first-generation Khmer immigrants continue to view "reality" in the new world through the lens of patterns of

meaning and relationships learned in their natal country. The
points of contact between Khmer culture and the larger American
society—what Smith calls junctures—form windows through
which we may view Cambodian culture as a process, both changing and restating itself as unchanging "tradition."

CHAPTER TWO

Khmer Literature
since 1975

Khing Hoc Dy

In April 1975, when Phnom Penh was taken by the Khmer Rouge, the entire urban population was evacuated. During the three years, eight months, and twenty days of the Pol Pot government, Khmer literature was paralyzed. Various poems of no literary importance and a "classical" prosodical form constantly addressed the same theme: peasant and agricultural development under the discerning direction of *ângka* (the party).[1] This contemporary literature attempted to show that the *ângka*'s agricultural and hydrological systems were superior to all those existing before then: "The new hydrological system has transformed our rice fields into modern rice fields, and has totally transformed the face of the Kampuchean countryside, in a way so miraculous that it has not been seen in two thousand years of history."[2] Revolutionary songs occupied a significant place in the literature of the Khmer Rouge regime and had an extremely important role in the radical revolution of this government. Here are two examples of songs: one is a national hymn of Democratic Kampuchea and the other a revolutionary song of the United National Front of Kampuchea:

Glorious April 17!

1. Ruby blood that sprinkles the towns and plains
   Of Kampuchea, our Homeland
   Splendid blood of workers and peasants,
   Splendid blood of revolutionary men and women soldiers!

2. This blood changes into implacable hatred
   And resolved war,
   April 17, under the flag of the Revolution.
   Freedom from slavery.

Refrain

   Live, Live, glorious April 17
   Glorious victory of greatest importance
   For the epoch of Angkor!

3. We come together to build
   A new Kampuchea and a new society
   Splendid and democratic in equality and justice,
   Steadfastly bestowing the heritage of independence,
       sovereignty
   And relying on our own strength.
   We resolutely defend
   Our Homeland, our sacred earth
   And our glorious Revolution!

Refrain

   Live, Live new Kampuchea
   Democratic and prosperous!
   We resolutely lift high
   The Red Flag of the Revolution,
   We build our Homeland,
   We cause her to progress in great leaps,
   In order to render her more glorious and more marvelous
       than ever![3]

The Red Flag of the Revolution

Our red flag is born from the blood of workers, peasants,
intellectuals, monks, youth, and women who
have sacrificed themselves to free our people.
There it is waving! gloriously!
Comrades, ahead! Smash the enemy!
There it is waving! gloriously!
Our implacable hatred toward the enemy embraces our heart.
There it is waving! gloriously!
We annihilate the imperialists, the reactionaries!
We scour the soil of Kampuchea!
Ahead! Ahead! We wrest victory![4]

Although in the revolutionary period in Kampuchea nothing of significant literary value was produced, Cambodian refugees abroad began to write between 1975 and 1979 and continue to do so, notably in France. Some young Khmer writers published their novels in the 1970s, for example, *Phka chhouk Kâmpŭchea* [Lotus flower of Cambodia], by Ing Kien (Paris, Edition Anakota, 1977, 120 pages), and *Kraoy Pél Phlieng* (After the rain), by Ros Viriya (Paris, Edition Angkor, 1979, 40 pages). Other Khmer authors abroad, however, encounter many difficulties in publishing their work. Ing Kien completed his second novel, *Pralĕung Neang Khemâra* (The soul of Miss Khemara), in 1977, but he has not been able to get it published. Biv Chhay Lieng, a well-known writer among Cambodians, finished his novel *Beh daung mae kântal sneh kâm* (The heart of the mother full of anguished love) in 1979, but succeeded in reaching the public only in 1989 because of technical and financial problems. These two novels describe the tragic life of Khmer families under Pol Pot. The literature of refugees abroad represents a continuity in modern Cambodian literature.

In Cambodia itself, a break in literary development was caused by the radical revolution of the Khmer Rouge, then by the 1978–79 Vietnamese invasion. From 1975 to 1979, no writer in Cambodia was able to express his reflections, ideas, or feelings, and no real literary work was created. But from 1979, Khmer literature has begun to revive, both abroad and in Cambodia itself.

Abroad, we find publications of Khmer literature, notably in France and Thailand. In France, several organizations produce works in Khmer. Cedoreck (Center for Documentation and Research on Khmer Civilization) has published (by offset press) several texts of classical and modern Khmer literature, books that had been published in Cambodia before 1975. Recently, Cedoreck printed a modern novel by a young author, Yim Pisal, titled *Sântŭh sneh knŏng phloeng sângkream* (The bonds of love during the flames of war; Paris, 1987). This novel shows us love between two soldiers in the resistance army fighting against the Vietnamese occupiers. The monthly journal, *Kaun Khmae,* founded by Cedoreck in 1983, has a cultural slant and contains short stories, especially by Pech Sangwawann, a long-time member of the Association

of Khmer Writers in Phnom Penh before 1975. The Stones of
Angkor Association (*Thmâ angko*) has also republished a number of Khmer texts, including classical works and modern novels.
As for modern poetry, Iv Huot, an academic, has published his
collection of poems, *Veasâna Ângko* (The destiny of Angkor).
All these poems, rich in metaphor, describe Angkor Wat and
Bayon, which symbolize Khmer cultural grandeur, with the aim of
assembling Cambodians of every persuasion to fight the army
from Hanoi.

In Thailand, several hundred extremely varied Cambodian textbooks have been published in Bangkok for distribution to Khmer
refugees in various camps by the Japan Sotoshu Relief Committee
with the cooperation of the United Nations High Commissioner
for Refugees. Among these publications are about forty modern
novels, stories, and legends, collections of sketches, and poems
written by refugees in the camps of Thailand. Such works often focus on the dramatic events between 1975 and 1979 under the
Khmer Rouge and the subsequent experiences under the Vietnamese occupation from 1979 to 1989 and a "cloak and sword" theme
inspired by Chinese epics. Suffering and nostalgia for the homeland are almost always represented in poems written by refugees.

In the United States in 1987, the Cambodia Foundation in
Texas, a part of the Khmer Association of the United States, organized a literary competition to encourage Cambodians to write
in their own language. Works included poems and short and full-
length novels. The principal themes were tragedy under the Pol Pot
regime, grief, separation from families or loved ones, and nostalgia
for Cambodia. Scientific and literary members of Cedoreck par-
ticipated as judges for this competition.

In Phnom Penh under the PRK, four principal organizations
produced literary works directed by the Communist party. First,
short stories were regularly found in the newspaper *Kâmpŭchea*
when it was edited by Khieu Kanharith. Serialized novels that succeeded with the public were then published as books.[5]

Second, the Institute of Sociology, Vĭccheasthan Sângkom
Vĭtyea, formerly directed by Vandy Kaon, counselor of state
(former student of the Faculty of Pedagogy and Faculty of Letters
in Phnom Penh University, 1965–70, and former student of the

Ecole Pratique des Hautes Etudes, IVth Section, Sorbonne, in
Paris) authored and edited several works: He wrote *Une réflexion
sur la littérature khmère,* in French (1981); and edited two volumes of collected Khmer stories and legends, with a printing of
4,200 for each volume (1987b). The body of these collections is
drawn from manuscripts and texts of publications by the former
Buddhist Institute (1969–70). Vandy Kaon has also written a
novel titled *Kaoh beysach* (The island of evil spirits; Phnom Penh,
1987a) describing a god-king, *tevâreach,* and life on an island under a despotic regime.

Third, the Ministry of Information and Culture, Krâsuong khô-
sânaka nĭng vobbâthŏa, directed by Pech Tum Krâvel, has issued
several works. *Yoeng btechnha lâh băng âvey âvey tĕang ăh
daoembey sângkrŭah cheat nĭng meatŏphoum* (We resolutely decide to make every sacrifice to save the nation and the motherland)
by Pèn Van Thôn (1983) describes the pathetic lives of men and
women soldiers of the revolutionary army in eastern Cambodia in
1978 who sacrificed their lives to fight against the Khmer Rouge to
save the nation and the homeland. *Măk Thoeung,* a play by Pech
Tum Krâvel (1983), depicts the unceasing battle by old Măk Thoeung against the petty king of Battambang. The author, responsible
for public relations at the ministry, revises the local history of this
region under Thai domination with the aims of attacking the
Khmer royalist system and Siamese imperialists and of showing
the beginning of ideas protesting despotism during the dark period
of Cambodian history.

Finally, a cultural publishing house, Ângka Baoh Pŭm Phsay
Vobbâthŏa, was established by the Ministry of Culture under the
minister Chheng Phon, former professor of dramatic art. It issues
ten thousand copies of each novel. Some representative novels are:
Phlieng rodauv ktav (Rain during the hot season) by Nonn Chan
(1986), *Thngai rĕah nôv phoum thmey* (the sun rises over a new
village) by Yok Kun (1986), and *Nĕak daoe kăt pyŭh* (Those who
cross the violent storm) by Kong Boun Chhoeun (1987a). These
novels describe the misfortunes and terror the country experienced
under the Khmer Rouge regime. Traumatized by the atrocities of
the latter, the authors have allowed little room in their accounts to
consider alterations in their cultural heritage. But from time to

time, the theme of Angkor and its glorious period appears in these publications with a specific goal: to fortify the heroic spirit of the revolutionary army, which must defend the party and the ancestral cultural heritage from American imperialists, Siamese colonialists (in these works the Vietnamese, allied with Phnom Penh, were no longer the target of authors), and reactionaries (Khing Hoc Dy 1989, 1992).

Constant themes in modern novels both inside Cambodia and abroad are the misfortunes and terror of the Pol Pot regime and the tragedy of life. But these themes are treated differently, according to the political tendencies of each author. Writers who were abroad during the period between 1975 and 1979 and after the drama of the Pol Pot regime depict fictional heroes entering the resistance army to fight the Khmer Rouge. From 1979 to the present, after the tragedy of life under Pol Pot and then the Vietnamese occupation, we find the heroes of novels enlisting in the liberation army to fight the army from Hanoi.

In literature produced in Cambodia, after the misfortunes and terror of the Khmer Rouge, the hero of the novel enlists in the revolutionary army to defend the homeland and rebuild the country under the clear-sightedness of the Communist party and along a socialist, Leninist-Marxist path (Khing Hoc Dy 1992). Khmer authors in Phnom Penh attempt to show us the differences between the Pol Pot regime and the new regime.

Under Pol Pot	Under the present Central Committee
all is dark like night (*yŭap*)	all is light like day (*thngai*)
lack (*khvâh*)	plenty (*bârĭbau*)
filthy (*krâkhŭăk*)	clean (*s'at*)
suffering (*tŭk sŏk*)	joy (*rik reay*)

They also show us smugglers and displaced refugees rallying to the army of the People's Republic of Kampuchea. The conception of art for art's sake has not existed in Phnom Penh since 1979. Art and literature must be in the service of the ideology of the Central Committee of the party and socialism.

The former minister of culture and information, Chheng Phon, was as a student favored by Hang Tun Hak (former rector of the Royal University of Fine Arts), who supervised all literary and artistic publications. The following is an extract from an unpublished project of reform drafted in French in 1957 by Chin Tong Lin, special secretary to Hang Tun Hak and friend of Chheng Phon:

I. Art as a vanguard element in national progress.
    1. The artist perceives what is, assists in realizing what does not yet exist.
    2. Importance of literature: absence of progressive literature and literature that leaves people thirsty for reading, but with a perfectly pure spirit. Hence a double danger: snobbery and disastrous political deviations can lead to the breakup of society or more practical and more economic means for popular education.
II. Acquired quality of a present-day Khmer literary work. Without allusion to general qualities that all works of art must possess and some of which we have noted in passing in preceding chapters, the characteristics appropriate to a good present-day Khmer literary work can be listed as follows: The subject must have a socialist leaning (socialist realism and progressive interpretation); the subject will thus be a portrait of present-day Khmer society, its evils, its struggles, its national values, the worth of the people. The interest in a piece is placed above all on struggle: the struggle of the oppressed against the oppressor, a struggle between generations, a struggle between new and old, and a struggle for the building of a new Cambodia.
    1. A variety of subjects and themes allow the avoidance of monotony.
    2. The work of art tends to educate some, but is not part of pedagogy. The work of art must in no case lose its primary characteristics: distraction, relaxation, emotion, original work, etc.
    3. A socialist tendency must never prevent us from constructing novels or plays with unfortunate ends. It is the general meaning that is included [sic], not only the plot. The process allows avoiding the boredom that ordinary people evidence when reading novels with messages: in reading the first pages, one already senses what the end must be.
    4. Do not hide the truth, even if it is disagreeable. The strength of a movement or a state is determined not only by its present situation, but also and above all by its aptitude for managing the future.

If the contents must be socialist and national, the presentation must remain Khmer: place, setting, action, language, song. . . . In modernizing, know how to preserve Khmer character, to remain Khmer; know how to adapt to the present; in the choice of translations, avoid rejecting or accepting a totality; know how to distinguish the fruit of misery from ignorance in general.
—in works inspired abroad (except for translations), know how to adapt without copying, to modernize without de-Khmerizing.
Form, in a restricted sense.
—The style must be lively, concise, direct, and above all it must be Khmer.

The new political orientation seems to appear clearly in all literary texts and was solemnly declared by Chheng Phon in 1988:

The people detest the Pol Pot regime, which has left an unsavory aftertaste in the spirit of the Cambodian people for social and political demagogy. The consciousness of the people remains petty bourgeois, impregnated with individualism and nationalism. The influence of Buddhism and the secular monarchical cult is much felt in the country. The complete building of a new society always takes into account that during the lifetime of a generation, several models of state are followed. The full blooming of culture and literature requires that everything out-of-date be rejected, choosing only elements of progressive and revolutionary art. Traditions that are tied to reactionary culture from the time of colonialism and imperialism must be destroyed.[6]

Between 1980 and 1989, several hundred Khmer literary texts have appeared in Cambodia and abroad. Modern Khmer literature is taking new ideological and cultural directions. Abroad, it undergoes strong influence from western literature and culture and takes great impetus from all literary genres. In Phnom Penh, it is managed by the machinery of the Communist party and increasingly diverges from that of the diaspora. The literature of the diaspora includes a great number of reprintings of texts published before 1975, while that in the People's Republic of Kampuchea and the State of Cambodia consists mostly of new works.

Two novels written between 1975 and 1989 illustrate some of these different tendencies; the first novel was written by a Khmer student in Paris, the second by a member of the party in Phnom Penh.

Phka chhouk Kâmpŭchea (Lotus flower of Cambodia) by Ing Kien (1977) recounts the history of a young woman, Kolap, whose existence—marked by karma—is beset with injury and misfortune. The first part of her life is tragic: during the war, and then two years under the club of the Khmer Rouge, she knew only deception, ordeal, and grief, having successively lost her mother, her small daughter, and her husband, whom she had married under family pressure. All died of hunger and sickness. The heroine, the only survivor, arrives in France thanks to Catholic Relief and rediscovers her former fiancé, Vidya, who had promised to join his life with hers. But now he is married. He nevertheless brings Kolap under his roof, with the consent of his wife, Ma Yan, a generous and understanding woman who wants above all to do a humanitarian act. In spite of former ties, the situation is clear. Vidya does not seduce Kolap because of his relationship with her is past history for him. The heroine does not accept this reality or the dependence in which she finds herself, and she wants to leave. But paradoxically, it is Ma Yan who sacrifices herself: one day she disappears.

After her departure, her husband succumbs to drinking and begs his former fiancée to look for his wife. One day the two women find themselves attending mass in a church were Ma Yan has taken refuge. Ma Yan finally agrees to rejoin her conjugal home to care for her husband, who is seriously ill. Kolap remains with them, henceforth considering Ma Yan as her sister and Vidya as her brother-in-law.

We note a striking fact in this novel, the intervention of the Catholic religion as the saving element: it is Catholic Relief that allows our heroine to escape hell; then she calls on God to find Ma Yan, who has herself taken refuge in a church to flee her problems. Ma Yan is also characterized by a completely Christian attitude: she receives Kolap into her house through charity, then leaves her husband in a spirit of sacrifice. The resignation of the masculine character is also striking: Vidya finds solace from his problems only in alcohol.

The second example, *Phlieng rodauv ktav* (Rain in the hot season) by Nonn Chan (1986), relates the heroic acts of soldiers in a revolutionary army fighting against reactionary soldiers, the Khmer Rouge, and the Siamese imperialists. The author notes in his foreword that he wrote this work as a response to "dear friends" with a thirst for reading who asked him to write in depth about the events of a new life under the leadership of a revolutionary party.

> "Rain in the hot season" is the revolutionary rain that allows the people to go beyond the danger of genocide, and gives birth to a brilliant and splendid new life.
>
> "Rain in the hot season" cleanses away the evil thoughts of misguided youth, and gives them a new consciousness, inciting them to enroll in the revolutionary army in order to build and defend their most dear homeland.
>
> "Rain in the hot season" is the victorious rain of the revolutionary army throughout the entire dry season. This is victory over the last post by the army harassed by Pol Pot, Ieng Sary, and Khieu Samphan, as well as reactionary battalions.

During the tenth anniversary of the People's Republic of Kampuchea, the revolutionary board of the city of Phnom Penh organized a literary and artistic competition with the aim of developing art and literature. The two novels that took first and second prize have since been published: *Ronôch phŏt haoey* (The waning moon has already passed), and *Choeng mékh thmey nai ktey sângkhĕum* (The new horizon of hope) both by Pal Vannariraks (1988a, 1988b).

Some older writers survived the bloodshed of the mid-1970s; four held responsible posts in the PRK government and played an important role in the development of contemporary Khmer literature: Chheng Phon (former minister of culture), Pech Tum Krâvel (vice-minister of information), Sâr Kapun (vice-minister of education), and Kong Boun Chhoeun (secretary general of the Association of Writers in Kampuchea). They have an important influence on young authors in Cambodia today and have encouraged them to compose novels, plays, and poems with an orientation to socialism and patriotism.

Table 1. Authors and literary works published in the Khmer language since 1975 (full citations appear in the References).

Overseas Publications

Published in Paris

Biv Chhay Lieng	1989	Mother's heart in the midst of anguished love
Ing Kien	1977	Lotus flower of Cambodia
Iv Huot	n.d.	The destiny of angkor
Ros Viriya	1979	After the rain
Yim Pisal	1987	The bonds of love in the flames of war

Published in Bangkok

Anonymous	1981	New poems from Srah Keo
Ching Sophon	1982a	Away from the homeland
Ching Sophon	1982b	The palace of death
Kil Samdol	n.d.	Kingdom of the thugs
Kim Phann Tara	1981	Vengeance
Lon Van	1981	The struggle in the first age
Nong Thierry	1982	In one life
Nong Thierry	n.d.	This is the fruit of your bad deeds
Taing Veng	1981	Your father is wrong, child

Publications in Cambodia (Phnom Penh)

Cambodia Ministry of Education	1976	Geography of Democratic Kampuchea
Cambodia, Ministry of Education	1982a	Collection of literary texts, 5th level
Cambodia, Ministry of Education	1982b	Collection of literary texts, 7th level
Cambodia, Ministry of Education	1984	Collection of literary texts, 6th level
Cambodia, Ministry of Education	1986	Revolutionary songs
Chheng Phon and Pech Tum Krâvel	1986	The march forward of the Cambodian Nation
Chhai Si Nariddh and Kusal Phirum	1986	The hero, Toch Phann
Chuon Men	1980	A view of the map of Cambodia during the Pol Pot–Ieng Sary period
Dao Noeu	1987	The violent storm of life
Hoe Sokhai	1984	The sun sets at Phal Village

Continued

Table 1. Continued

	Publications in Cambodia (Phnom Penh)	
Kèo Chanda	1983	The happiness of a peasant family
Khieu Kanharith, Chiva, and Khim Sarâng	1984	The Diamond of pailin—Meet after the rain has fallen—the last smile
Kim Pech Pinonn	1984	Uncle Kun, the peasant
Kim Pech Pinonn	1986	My heart
Kong Boun Chhoeun	1980	Flames of fire in the spirit
Kong Boun Chhoeun	1987a	Those who cross the violent storm
Kong Boun Chhoeun	1987b	The leaves fall from the trees
Nonn Chan	1983	The flower blossoms at dawn
Nonn Chan	1986	Rain in the hot season
Nonn Chan	1988a	Songs of life
Nonn Chan	1988b	The soul of Kesar Kol
Pal Vannariraks	1988a	The new horizon of hope
Pal Vannariraks	1988b	The waning moon has already passed
Pech Tum Krâvel	1983	Mak Thoeng
Pèn Vann Thôn	1983	We resolutely decide to make every every sacrifice to save the nation and the motherland
Pèn Vann Thôn	1987	Remembrance of winter
Pèn Vann Thôn	1988a	The Moonlight across the frontier
Pèn Vann Thôn	1988b	The story of a crow and the fish
Pok Ponn So Mach	1988	Darkness in broad daylight
Pol Saroeung	1988	The faithful heart
Sam Sophâl	1986a	Springtime
Sam Sophâl	1986b	The scar
Sam Sophâl	1987	Nocturnal animals
Sam Sophâl	1988	The ties of young love
Sar Sapun	1982	Collection of poems
Sar Kapun and Yok Lun	1985	The poet's heart
Sâr Sieng Hieng	1987	The last cartridge
Ti Chi Huot	1984	Return to our home
Ti Chi Huot	1988	A moonless sky
Vandy Kaon	1987a	The island of evil spirits
Vann Chantha	1984	The children with a magical pencil
Yao Sam Phon	1988	Stop crying, my love
Yok Kun	1984	The life of suffering during the Pol Pot–Ieng Sary period
Yok Kun	1986	The Sun rises over New Village
Yok Kun	1987	Suffering from being lost
You Bo and B. Vuddh	1986	The Group of children of the magical gourd

CHAPTER THREE

Khmer Traditional Music Today

Sam-Ang Sam

Because Cambodia has not yet produced many music historians or ethnomusicologists, a comprehensive history of Khmer music is not available. Moreover, art, particularly music, is still a low priority in Cambodia compared to other areas of study such as politics. When one writes history, one writes political history, a policy that echoes the old cliché that "country must be first before art can grow." But alongside politics, art and culture must also survive to play a vital part in the present attempt to restore and rebuild the Khmer nation.

Various outside observers with an interest in Khmer culture have poorly assessed Cambodia's current political and cultural situation. Foreigners studying the arts in Cambodia usually concentrate on the University of Fine Arts in Phnom Penh and assume that what they see and hear there is representative of Khmer culture. They do not realize that the university is not only an educational institution but a center for experimentation, creation, development, modernization, reform, modification, and production. One must also go outside the university to the villages to study Khmer culture: to examine, for example, masked dance (*lkhaon khaol*), shadow plays (*sbaek*), *basăk* theater (*lkhaon basăk*), *yike* theater (*yike*), and alternate singing (*ayai*). For a more complete survey, one must also study the past and use it as a point of reference for looking at the present and projecting into the future.

In this chapter, I examine the present state of traditional Khmer music both in Cambodia and in the United States in relation to the political shifts of 1975, a date that marks a pivotal point for present-day Khmer music. This study is based on historical, political, and ethnomusicological writings, video productions, audio cassettes, interviews with Khmer musicians, private documents provided by recent visitors to Cambodia, and my own observations and assessment of Khmer music in-the-making both in asylum and resettlement countries as well as in Cambodia itself during recent trips.

As with most other Asian cultures, music is passed on through oral tradition. There are essentially six types of ensembles: *arĕak ka, kong skor, pĭn pĕat, mohôri, yike,* and *basăk. Arĕak ka* has been considered the most traditional of Khmer ensembles and is utilized for spirit worship and wedding ceremonies. Its instrumentation consists of the *tro khmae* (three-stringed fiddle), *khsae muoy* (musical bow or monochord), *chapey dâng vaeng* (long-necked lute), *pey brâhŏs* (double-reed shawn) and *skor arĕak* (goblet drums). *Kong skor* is a funeral ensemble comprised of a *srâlai khlâng khaek* (quadruple-reed oboe), *peat* (a straight frame or row of eight bossed gongs), *kong kraol* (large suspended gong), and *skor thŭm* (large barrel drum) (Sam 1988:23).

Pĭn pĕat is the ensemble traditionally accompanying the *lkhaon kbăch* (court dance), *lkhaon khaol* (masked dance), *sbaek* (shadow play), and religious ceremonies. It consists of *srâlai* (quadruple-reed oboes), *roneat* (xylophone), *kong vŭang* (circle of gongs), *sâmphô* (small barrel drum), *skor thŭm* (large barrel drum), and *chhing* (small cymbals). *Mohôri* is an entertainment ensemble that accompanies a play of the same name and Khmer folk dances. It consists of *roneat, khlŏy* (duct flute), *tro* (two-stringed fiddle), *krâpoe* (three-stringed floor zither), *thon romonea* (two-piece drum set), and *chhing.*

Yike is a folk ensemble that accompanies a play of the same name. It is comprised of *tro ou cămhieng* (a two-stringed fiddle made from a coconut shell), and several *skor yike (yike* drums). *Basăk* is also an ensemble used to accompany a play of the same name. It is comprised of *tro ou basăk* (half-coconut shell, two-stringed fiddle), *khĕum* (hammered dulcimers), *păn* (woodblock), *skor basăk (basăk* drums), *chhap* (cymbals), and *kong kraol.*

During the so-called Funan and Chenla periods in the region now known as Cambodia, from the first to the eighth centuries, elements of Khmer traditional beliefs were incorporated into the newly adopted Hinduism. This syncretism of belief and ritual is preserved in peasant society today. Music plays an extremely important role in these beliefs.

The religious and artistic complex of Angkor was the most glorious achievement of Khmer history, between the ninth and the fifteenth centuries. Gigantic masterpieces grace its compound, symbolizing the union of celestial and earthly beings. We can see *âbsara* carved on the walls of the great temples built in the vicinity of Angkor. These celestial nymphs hold musical instruments: the *pǐn* (harp), *srâlai, kong vǔang, skor yôl* (suspended barrel drum), *sâmphô* (small barrel drum), *skor thǔm, chhing,* and *kong thǔm* (large suspended gong). The instruments and the composition of ensembles of present-day Khmer music are similar to those we see represented on the bas-reliefs of Angkor. We thus have every reason to believe that present-day Khmer musical forms are the living continuation of the musical tradition of the ancient Khmer.

Khmer power diminished following the Angkor era. In 1432, Angkor was looted by the Siamese, then abandoned as Khmer kings and the musicians of their courts fled. The complex was later overrun by vegetation (Delvert 1983:34). The capital was moved to Longvek, but once again, in 1593, the Longvek capital was sacked by the Siamese (Sam 1987:2). Following the decline of the Khmer empire, music and its functions were very much affected, and a new style of melancholy, sentimental music emerged.

The period 1796–1859 was a renaissance for Khmer music. Especially after King Ang Duong ascended the throne in 1841 in the capital at Oudong, Khmer music and other art forms were revived and again began to flourish (Sam 1987:2, 1988:18). The twentieth century, until 1975, was a period of conservation for Khmer traditional arts, as ancient art forms were retained and carefully preserved under the watchful eyes o the elders and master artists.

The genocidal regime of Pol Pot (1975–79) claimed over a million Khmer lives; artists and musicians were not exempted. In 1979 the *Kampuchea Review* claimed: "Out of 190 ballet artists, only 40 escaped death under the Pol Pot–Ieng Sary regime" (1979:H1). Three years later, after accepting the position of minister of information and culture, Chheng Phon announced, "The genocidal Pol Pot–Ieng Sary–Khieu Samphan regime destroyed our national culture almost completely and killed almost 80 percent of our male and female performers" (*Kampuchea Review* 1982:H1). Presenting a similar account, Clayton Jones writes, "Some 90 percent of classical dancers died or were killed in the late 1970s under the Communist Khmer Rouge regime, which tried to wipe out the country's traditional culture" (1987:1). Susan Pack, one of a group of journalists who traveled to Cambodia, cites Chheng Phon as saying, "We have 10 percent teachers or professors after the destruction. Ninety percent were gone. There were 380,000 artists and intellectuals. During Pol Pot, just 300 people survive" (1989:J4).

This slaughter has resulted in a severe shortage of artists and musicians, both as teachers and performers. Inside Cambodia, survivors have tried to regroup former artists and musicians, as well as to restore the few documents that have survived Khmer Rouge destruction. In a country in which the government and its populace are constantly threatened by warfare, the reformation and modification of culture, including the arts, is inevitable. Nevertheless, the essential structure remains, although content changes. Many performances and their themes were adjusted to suit the political ideology of the Communist party.

Another constraint faced by Khmer musicians in Cambodia is the scarcity of literary documents, the result of the burning of libraries and other important centers of primary sources during the Khmer Rouge period. And the PRK government removed books, magazines, audio tapes and records, and movies that brought back memories of preceding regimes.[1]

Throughout the 1980s, Cambodia was under a state of emergency. Travel was restricted, thus limiting artistic exposure. Before 1975 the arts reached audiences of every class in society; the University of Fine Arts in Phnom Penh had organized several performing tours each year, taking artistic productions to villages throughout the country, even to remote areas.

Yet the arts are resurging. Pack writes, "There is growth. The number of theaters in Phnom Penh has jumped from three to 15. There are 250 theater groups in the country. Traditional music is

being played, and traditional dances are being performed"
(1989:J4).

The School of Fine Arts (in University of Fine Arts), which
was reopened in 1981 under the direction of Chheng Phon, has
taken responsibility for preserving Khmer culture. In the 1960s,
the university had sent teams of researchers to various regions
throughout the country to collect and study indigenous folk
dances and popular theater forms: *yike* theater and *basăk* theater.
Lkhaon khaol (masked dance) and *sbaek thŭm* (large-sized
shadow play) teachers and performers were brought to the university to serve residencies. Modifications then occurred to some extent, but not for public performances. During wartime, changes
and alterations had been made to suit the political thrust of the
current regime. The *basăk* theater presented revolutionary pieces,
while *yike* performers sang the praises of the Vietnamese saviors
(Martin 1986:5–11).

Available written materials, audio tapes, and movies tell us that
most of the former master musicians died during the genocide and
war of 1975–79. The repertoires today are shortened, the performance is less refined, and musical instruments are scarce. To conform to political demands, students learn new models. They have a
different kind of understanding of their music than did their parents or older brothers and sisters. They have lost their traditional
values and must come to grips with political ones. The artistic
ideal in traditional Khmer art can no longer be practiced when
faced with this kind of threat. The arts that were created and
performed for national, traditional, and recreational purposes
with didactic and artistic impulses are replaced by political and
revolutionary themes presented as propaganda. The arts that used
to be free, conservative, and expressive are now often dictated
from above.

Meanwhile, Khmer arts have undergone additional change
among emigrant populations abroad. Among the approximately
150,000 Khmer refugees now living in the United States, for example, there has been no formal schooling in Khmer artistry. A
few organizations, such as the Khmer Studies Institute, the
Cambodian-American Heritage, and the Cambodian Studies Center in the United States, and the Centre de Documentation et de

Recherche sur la Civilisation khmère (Cedoreck) in France have
begun to provide such programs.

With regard to traditional music beyond the borders of Cambodia, Khmer experience different problems, not political but
artistic. The shortage of musicians and musical instruments are
the major problems in the preservation of traditional Khmer
musical culture. There has been substitution and intermingling
as well as reduction in the musical instrumentation of ensembles.
Student musicians are learning in new ways, using tapes and
records rather than learning directly from a master. This approach
results in a limited repertoire as well as musical mutations of original pieces.

Khmer youngsters praise and then adopt western music, particularly "pop" music, and discredit their own. They are saturated by
Music Television (MTV), which broadcasts only western popular
music. As a music teacher of Khmer children, I have noticed that
my students come to class with an attitude of being "American"
and not "Khmer." They prefer to conduct their conversations in
English. Asked what musical instruments they want to play, they
replay "guitar, keyboard, drum set." Asked whether or not they
want to learn how to sing Khmer songs, most reply "No!" In my
music-appreciation class, I play Khmer music with several types of
Khmer ensembles; Khmer youth find these pieces "slow" and
"boring." During breaks, they form small groups, some singing
rap music and doing break dancing, while others imitate dance
movements seen on *Soul Train* and *Dance Fever.* No one dances a
Khmer dance or sings a Khmer song.

Needless to say, Khmer children who are committed to learning
Khmer music are scarce. These attitudes and behaviors are the result of a lack of understanding and appreciation of Khmer traditional values. We Khmer living beyond the borders of our country
cannot compete with the musical acculturation of our young.
Traditional Khmer music loses its audience, its full range of repertoire, instrumentation, and performance and becomes virtually
symbolic.

A new development in Khmer musical form can be observed
outside Cambodia. We Khmer have not been able to form a complete *pĭn pĕat* ensemble, which is needed for various ceremonies.

In performances, Khmer musicians (myself included) both consciously and unconsciously borrow instruments from other Khmer ensembles and mix them with those of the *pǐn pěat*. Because of the scarcity and distribution of musicians and musical instruments, this borrowing is difficult to avoid. In addition, Khmer traditionally hold great respect for elders. In performance situations, we cannot tell our older musicians (or even younger ones) not to play with us just because they do not know how to play a *pǐn pěat* instrument. Moreover, excluding them from the group would reduce the ensemble even further, thus making it impossible to produce a full accompaniment. Worst of all, discouraging other musicians from playing might be seen as a break in the continuity of Khmer musical life.

In the United States, Khmer refugees must cope with social, economic, and cultural adjustments. It is easier for the young, more difficult for those who are older. First, there is a language barrier; second, an awareness of traditional values is greater for the older generation than for the younger. Old folks remember their traditional customs and past experiences. Religious and traditional ceremonies, attended predominantly by the older people, are held in various Khmer communities, where they provide psychological relief from depression and homesickness. As traditional activities continue to be practiced, although to a lesser extent than in Cambodia, Khmer music continues to play its usual role. It is heard during the New Year's celebration, at weddings, and, most prominently, in dance and theater performances.

Although we Khmer are far from home, our national holidays, like the New Year, in April are always celebrated. From the thirteenth to the fifteenth of April of each year, Khmer communities gather to celebrate. We go to the pagoda to pray, offer food to the monks, and listen to them chant. Some Khmer play traditional games, and in the evening we go to traditional dance and theater performances, which are accompanied by traditional Khmer music. Most Khmer also hold traditional weddings, although they celebrate them in a much simplified form: a ceremony that formerly lasted three days and three nights is now performed in a day, during which *phléng ka* (wedding music) is played almost continuously.

In this new environment under radically changed conditions, Khmer traditions are changing. Ceremonies that traditionally included music now do not, for instance, the *bŏn phka* (fund-raising "flower" ceremony) and *bŏn phchŭm bĕn* (soul day).

In Cambodia, Khmer musicians did not conform to strict work schedules. In fact, there was no such schedule for many of them. They spent much of their time practicing and playing whenever they had free time and felt like doing so, perhaps in the evening after dinner at home. In the United States, most Khmer musicians are obliged to work a forty-hour week doing manual labor. Evenings and weekends are for recuperating in order to return to work, where schedules seldom vary. Dedicated Khmer musicians, however, make the time to practice and perform. In their new environment they usually perform in concert and at dance and theater performances.

Despite new social, economic, and cultural realities and an exposure to modern technology, Khmer musicians attempt to preserve their musical tradition and maintain their identity. Their playing style remains faithful to their traditions. Because they have lost their country, land, family, tradition, and culture, they are not easily swayed by new things. Rather, they hold onto their traditions, desiring to impart their values to the younger generation and working fervently to do so.

Khmer experience of popular music also continues to change. Among community activities, the most popular and frequent is the casual social gathering, usually involving social dancing accompanied by a so-called rock band. Khmer rock bands are found in many Khmer-American communities and these bands use western instruments such as electric guitars, electric basses, keyboards, and drum sets. As the music is intended for dancing, the bands play western popular songs composed by various groups and artists such as the Beatles, the Rolling Stones, the Bee Gees, Lionel Richie, Michael Jackson, Van Halen, Rod Stewart, and Madonna. But they also play Khmer popular songs set to Khmer rhythms—*rŏam vŭang, rŏam kbăch,* and *saravăn*—as well as to western rhythms, such as bolero, cha cha, slow, and madison. These dance gatherings are attended mostly by the young. Audio cassettes of Khmer popular songs can be found in every Khmer store. The production of Khmer popular music in the United States grows much faster than in Cambodia than it ever has, even during the prewar period. Its growth is due to its popularity among Khmer youth, who are willing to pay for such entertainment, and to the accessibility of affordable modern equipment.

This interest in popular music is not strange at all. The majority of Americans listen to rock and roll, not to classical music. Indians listen to Indian film music rather than Hindustani or Carnatic music, while the majority of Thai prefer popular music to the *pi phat, mohôri,* or *khruang sai*. It is sad and unfortunate to see things go this way, but it is reality. Traditional music is restricted to a small number of people, particularly the elderly. All Khmer traditional music shares this fate.

The processes of preserving and developing traditional Khmer music occur only within Cambodia, the environment in which Khmer is purely Khmer and musicians can afford the time needed to practice the arts and music. Outside Cambodia, the contexts in which music is fostered have changed. As the older generation of musicians dies, traditional music subsides because the young lack understanding and appreciation of their traditional culture and thus do not see the need to carry on their precious legacy.

James Brandon remarked at the annual meetings of the Association of Asian Studies in Washington, D.C., in 1989, "Performing arts do not die, but performers do. As long as there are artists to perform the arts, they will survive." This is precisely the case: 80 to 90 percent of Khmer musicians are reported to have died or have been killed during the past decade and a half. We are consequently short of musicians who would enable this tradition to live. We are also concerned not only with the preservation of Khmer arts but with the generation gap—the emphasis on quality over quantity, and walking forward rather than backward.

In short, when little attention is paid to the arts, artists fall victim to political consequences. The social and musical changes discussed in this chapter are the result and reflection of political shifts and chaos in Cambodia since 1975. We have lost so much. We have lost our most able musicians, artists who have devoted their entire lives to gaining knowledge and ability. Now they are gone.

CHAPTER FOUR

The Revival of Masked Theater, *Lkhaon Khaol,* in Cambodia

William Lobban

Lkhaon khaol is the masked theater of Cambodia presenting the story of the *Ramayana,* in which Rama's wife Sita is abducted by Ravana. Traditionally it has been performed by troupes of male dancers; all roles, even those of women, are played by men. The same man often plays the same role for many years.

Although this form of theater was not performed all over Cambodia, it was well known in the provinces near Phnom Penh, where there were two villages with resident companies. There were also troupes in Siemreap and Battambang. At one time in Battambang there was a female troupe, but there are few written details about it (Sam 1988). The male troupe of Battambang was very well known, and the text of the performance was recorded by Française Bizot during the 1960s (1981).

The village of Wat Sviey Andet (Vât Svay Ântaet), eight kilometers downstream from Phnom Penh on the Mekong River, was the home of one of the best-known *lkhaon khaol* troupes in the country.[1] This village had a large troupe of performers resident either in the village or in nearby hamlets. Traditionally, the first roles of the boy performers were the simpler monkey (*sva*) roles of onlookers at the court of Rama rather than the more exacting roles of the monkey warriors. Over the years, various boys would begin performing the more complicated warrior roles. They would at times assume roles as the giants (*yĕak*) in Ravana's army, but it was more common for performers to continue in the roles for which they were initially trained. If a performer did change roles, he usually remained in that character because each character has its own dance steps.

The troupe at Wat Sviey Andet traditionally performed the *lkhaon khaol* at the time of the Khmer New Year Festival. This falls in April, when the village is waiting for the commencement of the rainy season, which usually occurs during late May or early June. There is little agricultural activity in the village during this period, as the paddies are bare and the tobacco crop, which is the main cash crop at Wat Sviey Andet, does not require much attention from the farmers. This is traditionally a time when people either look for other work or repair their houses and agricultural implements, so that the time spent in rehearsal of the *lkhaon khaol* during February, March, and early April does not interfere much with the agricultural life of the village. The little work that is carried on at this time is usually done by women, and they are not involved with the performance except to act as dressers for the dancers.

Lkhaon khaol always presents the *Ramayana* story, usually performed over several evenings. The story is narrated by three or four people situated to the side of the performing area, while the actors act out the story being told (see Figure 1). These performers never dance during the narration; rather, they dance, accompanied by music, so as to alternate with the narration. Much of the narration is chanted, but individual narrators speak the dialogue for the various characters. This dialogue is always enhanced by the beating of the bass drum, *skor*.

A chief narrator always runs the entire performance. He sets the pace of the performance by controlling the dialogue and giving instructions to the musicians who play the *skor*.

The orchestra used for the *lkhaon khaol* is a Khmer type called *pĭn pĕat*, with the difference that more prominence is given to the role of the bass drum, the *skor*, than is usual for this type of orchestra. The orchestra is occasionally increased in size by the addition of an extra *roneat* (xylophone), but with metal keys. This xylophone is in addition to the two that have rosewood and bamboo keys respectively (Sam 1988). The *skor* plays an important role in the performance and appears to be used both to emphasize

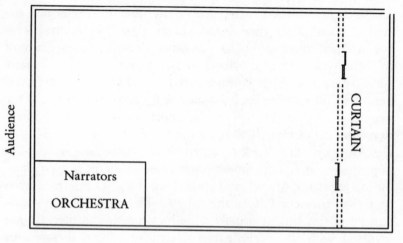

Figure 1. Stage setting for *lkhaon khaol*

the dialogue and to cue the dancers to take up their positions for performing the various dances. The dances portray either the battles or journeys of the characters played by the dancers.

The text of the *Ramayana* used by the Wat Sviey Andet troupe was previously housed in the monastery situated on the edge of the village. Sem Sara (1967) reports that it was written in both palm-leaf manuscripts and school exercise books. By 1990, none of these remained; the vât was used as a detention center from 1975 to 1979, during the Pol Pot period. The last prewar performance was in 1969, and the *Ikhaon* text is now remembered by only one of the seven survivors of the original troupe. He had chanted the text many times and retains a clear memory of it. He has, in turn, taught portions of this text to two other villagers, who now assist him with the performance.

The seven survivors of the original troupe are now all over sixty years of age. They had all played a variety of roles, but each had a preference for a certain role he had performed for a number of years. All had begun to learn their respective roles when they were between twelve and fifteen years of age and apparently continued to play those characters over the years. Two men who later performed as monkeys began as "green monkeys" when they were boys. These are clown roles, and they appear to provide much of the entertainment, which involves bawdy gestures.

The oldest informant, who is now seventy-three, performed the role of Ravana for many years. He was the recognized *lkhaon* master of the village, and Cambodians report that only the best dancers were taught this role. The gestures for the Ravana role are quite different from those for the other roles and can be learned only after the performer has mastered a subordinate role. This elderly informant had first danced the role of a Chan, one of Ravana's warriors, but he was selected at an early age to study the role of Ravana when he was recognized as having special dancing ability.

By 1980, all the performing soloists in the village had been killed or had fled to the Cambodian-Thai border camps. There are some eight dancers now in their forties, however, who had played subordinate roles in the performance before 1969, when the last complete *lkhaon khaol* was performed. They began to teach the *lkhaon* roles to the younger men as early as 1982, but the village had neither the necessary costumes nor the money to perform the dance drama, and there was no serious attempt to revive the art until 1990. The older dancers gave basic instruction to the younger men, but because there was no possibility of performing, this instruction was intermittent and was not taken with any seriousness by the young people in the village.

The *lkhaon khaol* performance I observed at Wat Sviey Andet in April 1990 was the first full-scale performance held in the village since 1969, and it was made possible by the generosity of the Department of Arts in the Ministry of Culture and the personal interest of the minister, Chheng Phon. The minister arranged with the military authorities that all the young men involved with the performance were to be exempt from any form of military service during the rehearsal and performance period. This exemption allowed the older men to work with the same group of males without interruption for three months before the performance.

The men involved were also paid a token wage by the Ministry of Culture as an incentive for their participation in the performance and to encourage them to think of themselves as semiprofessionals, as had the troupe in the 1960s. Although the wage was only the equivalent of two American dollars, this amount is significant in a society where cash payments are rare for villagers.

The performance took place in the evening on the edge of the village, beside the Mekong River. A pavilion had been erected over a rectangular area measuring twenty by twenty-five meters and surrounded by bamboo railings. One of the narrower ends was hung with curtains; the dancers waited behind these between entrances. Two appertures were made in the curtains, from which all entrances and exits were made. The orchestra was seated down the long side of the pavilion, to the right, within the performing area, while the three narrators sat in front or beside of them.

The public was held back from the performing area by a bamboo rail seventy-five centimeters above the ground. This rail was more a demarcation line than an actual boundary, since it did not stop children from wandering through the performing area and gradually encroaching on the performance space. The children were chased back from time to time, but no real measures were made to keep them out of the stage area.

The bamboo rail on the left side of the performance area was quite thick, providing an important prop during the acting out of the story. Whenever the court of either Rama or Ravana entered the performing area, they went to the rail and adopted various poses while sitting on it. The major characters, such as Rama or Ravana, faced away from the curtains, while the remainder of the court sat sideways facing the major character. Occasionally, when there was dialogue between one of the generals and the major character, the general or Hanuman stood in front of everyone gesturing in an exaggerated manner as the narrator on the other side of the performing space presented the dialogue. It was while the dancers were seated on this rail that the monkeys provided most of the groundling entertainment.

Seats directly opposite the draped curtains were reserved for important visitors and officials whom the village wished to impress. Most of the audience, numbering between three and five hundred, were seated on the sides of the performing space. The audience was continually shifting, with people coming and going at will. Children were allowed to wander through the proceedings as they wished, and as the evening performance progressed, they fell asleep where they had been sitting, oblivious to the drama being performed in front of them or the movement of the crowd behind them. In addition, numerous comments were made by the audience throughout the performance, quite in contrast to a western performance where the audience remains seated and quiet.

The costumes for this performance were lent to the village by the Ministry of Culture's Department of Arts. These were costumes no longer being used for classical ballet. Masks for all the dancers were also supplied by the Department of Arts. The village had previously owned many of the masks needed for such a performance and needed to rent only the elaborate headpieces, *mkŏd,* worn by Sita and her maid and Rama and his brother Laksmana, but all the village's masks disappeared after 1972. Many of these masks are made from papier-maché, and they would have disintegrated or been eaten by vermin without proper storage.

The only unmasked characters were Rama and Laksmana, in addition to the two women, Sita and her maid, played by boys who even out of costume adopted mincing and exaggerated feminine gestures and walk. There were two actors in the role of ordinary people, periodically performing as clowns and prop bearers. These two were often the butt of crude jokes, also displaying exaggerated and bawdy gestures to the more evil characters of the drama. One of these actors was slightly crippled by a turned-in foot, making his dance movements somewhat grotesque. This role is apparently often filled by crippled actors, and while performing they themselves make a joke of their clumsiness.

These two characters later played other small roles, including that of a bird attacking one of Ravana's generals. One clown actor appeared with a *kroma,* a long cotton scarf, the ends in each of his hands and the middle portion covering his head. This he used as his wings. On another occasion, one of the clowns entered carrying a small tree and appeared to be moving it around the performing area so that one of the *yĕak* giants in Ravana's army could use neither the tree nor the fruit it supposedly carried. These two

characters also entered the performing space at will to clear the
space of any leaves or fruit that had fallen during the previous
scene. They adopted no special pose or step to do so, but entered
in the usual way. It was almost as though they were not on stage;
the action continued in their presence as if no one on stage could
see them.

The only character who actually spoke his own lines was Ěsey,
the holy hermit who befriends Sita when she is banished to live in
the jungle. Although the dancer wore a full mask, he lifted the
mask when he spoke his lines so that it sat tipped back on his head.
The two clown figures accompanied him, but at times seemed to
mock his supposed age and infirm movements.

The two women's roles were played by boys, who either adopted
a feminine stance most of the time, both on and off the stage, or
were by nature more feminine than other boys in the village. These
two characters did not actually dance, but only entered behind the
major male character; they adopted a kneeling submissive pose,
then sat on the side rail. They were never involved with the dance
action, always exiting at the conclusion of the dialogue before the
dancing began.

The performance I witnessed at Wat Sviey Andet told a portion
of the *Ramayana* story involving battles and intrigues to recapture
Sita after she was abducted by Ravana. The play opened with Sita
already in captivity in Ravana's palace. Sita was never seen in the
company of Rama, and appeared only when Ravana assembled his
court to plan his next battle with Rama.

The evening was divided into two parts, the first beginning at
about 5 P.M. and running until 7:15 P.M. There was then a break,
and the audience went to eat. The performance then resumed
at 9:30 P.M. and continued until 12:30 A.M. The performance
was only one portion of the *lkhaon khaol,* and we were told
that a performance of the whole text would take from six to ten
evenings, depending on the length of the dance sequences being
performed.

The battle scenes between Hanuman's (the monkey king) soldiers (the monkeys), and Ravana's soldiers (the *yĕak*) exhibited different movements for the two groups of characters. The *yĕak*
adopted heroic poses, strutting around the performing area. Their

movements were exaggerated, especially during their marching and combat stances. In contrast, the monkeys were much more agile and, of course, included scratching, which reduced their roles to something very commonplace in the eyes of the spectators. When the two groups encountered one another and then engaged in battle, the contrast of the exaggerated pose of the *yĕak* to the more athletic and comic stance of the monkeys was very evident.

The younger boys playing the roles of green monkeys were usually on stage only when Rama's court was assembled. They utilized a monkey-like walk, moving primarily on bent legs and propelling themselves along with their hands. They provided comic relief to the high drama being enacted. Most of their activity seemed to involve picking for fleas on either their own or their neighbors' bodies. Later in the performance, the flea-picking became increasingly outrageous, often involving groping around in other monkey's crotches.

They became involved in the action of the play only when one of Ravana's generals attempted to set up an altar with offerings to attract the Ĕsey. The green monkeys spend most of their time destroying the offerings, so that in the end the general's efforts failed. Since the green monkeys were adopting many of the movements of real monkeys, they were greeted with numerous calls and shouts from the audience.

The performance was strongly and at times violently gestured, in strong contrast to the classical ballet performance of the same story. Here in the *lkhaon khaol* are the battles and epic journeys, during which all the action and fighting that occur is being related. In the classical ballet performance there seems to be greater concentration on the subterfuge and subtleties of the story, and the actual abduction of Sita and the magic used to lure Rama and Lakmana away so that Ravana can attempt to work his magic on Sita are shown.

In the *lkhaon khaol* performed at Wat Sviey Andet, these scenes are described through dialogue, but battles and journeys that involve locating Sita and plans to try to free her are depicted in dance. At times it appeared that this performance was a contrast to that of the classical ballet: it was the other side of the story, the violent masculine side as opposed to the subtle and feminine side.

This difference may be attributed to the fact that Khmer classical ballet has always been danced by women. It is only since the 1950s that men have been included in classical ballet. The roles that men perform in classical ballet are those actually taken from the *lkhaon khaol;* they perform the monkey roles, roles that are a force for good.

The overall strength of the *lkhaon khaol* and the rustic setting of its performance sets it, both literally and metaphorically, outside the royal palace setting of Khmer classical ballet. It can be seen that both are derived from the same traditional source, but because one is based in the village and is performed by semiprofessionals and men as opposed to full professionals and women in formal theatrical settings, there are these marked differences.

The performance of *lkhaon khaol* at Wat Sviey Andet was not smooth. The director, a former dancer and now a professor of dance at the School of Fine Arts in Phnom Penh, actually had to walk on stage several times to change the position of the dancers and to advise them on when to exit—occurrences never seen in classical dance performances. There was an explicitness to the performance that made it far more accessible to the villagers than the ballet would have been. Although they were familiar with the story they were better able to follow the plot in a more basic form.

In a classical dance performance, the narration is usually sung while the dancers perform, and a viewer must have some sophistication to follow the subtlety of the words and gestures simultaneously. In *lkhaon khaol,* there is complete separation between the two kinds of performances, for dance is performed in alternation to the narration. In the spring of 1990 at Wat Sviey Andet, there was also much more audience involvement than I have seen at the classical ballet, in that they commented on the dancing and at times actually took part in the battles by shouting and going on stage. For this village audience, the *lkhaon khaol* was not a sophisticated exercise but a vivid and immediate event involving a familiar and very Cambodian story.

CHAPTER FIVE

Cambodian Buddhist Monasteries in Paris: Continuing Tradition and Changing Patterns

Milada Kalab

Theravada Buddhism is an integral part of Khmer ethnicity and as such has special significance for refugees. Like any religion, it gives meaning to the life of its followers and solace in times of special need. As an aspect of ethnicity, it provides one of the markers by which the in-group is identified. To outsiders, Khmers emphasize that Buddhism is a world religion, making them part of a well-known civilization. Among themselves they are aware of the subtle differences between their own practices and those of Buddhists of other countries, giving them a unique identity.

Although Buddhism teaches impermanence and the constant change of all phenomena, its doctrine acts as an anchor in the flux of life. And through continued practice of their own folk religion, Khmer refugees aspire to a special kind of constancy, trying to recreate and revive the rituals and decorations as they were in Cambodia in the 1960s, an impossible task in the physical and social climate of Paris. The resulting modifications affect many areas of traditional religion, including adaptations in the location of monks, the establishment and operation of monasteries, and the performance of ceremonies.

A Buddhist society needs monks who personify the ideal way of life, provide the best opportunity for their followers to acquire merit, and perform the necessary ceremonies. When Phnom Penh fell, there was just one Khmer monk in Paris, Venerable Yos Huot, who was studying there for an advanced degree. When refugee monks arrived from Thailand, Cambodian laymen found a flat for them, and in 1980 a house was bought in Créteil, a southeastern suburb of Paris. This site became Wat Khemâraram (Vât Khemâraram), where a temple was built in the garden in more or less traditional Khmer architectural style. It was consecrated in 1985. The founding of this first monastery in Paris is described in detail by Ang Chouléan (1981), whose informant was Venerable Buer Kry, the chief monk when the move to Créteil was made.

After four months, several other monasteries were established. Venerable Yos Huot moved to his hermitage in Fontainebleau. Venerable Chou Kim Tan accepted an invitation from local Cambodians to settle in Rennes, and Venerable Touch Sarith moved in the same way to Bordeaux. The monks remaining in Créteil expressed discontent there, so in 1982 a group of supporters rented an inexpensive house for them, and this was the beginning of Wat Bodhivansa (Vât Pôthi Vuăng) in Bagneux, another southeastern suburb of Paris. Venerable Buer Kry remained alone in Créteil, and he invited two Cambodian refugee monks to come from Thailand. They later deserted him to join Wat Bodhivansa. He then ordained some young monks, but as of 1985 most resident monks were non-Cambodians, although exact numbers are not available.

At Bagneux, the monks began with an egalitarian organization reminiscent of the early historical community of Buddhist monks before hierarchies developed. But life at the Bagneux temple became chaotic, and the monks thus agreed that someone should be in charge. Venerable Sar Sastr agreed to be the chief monk. Wat Bodhivansa was located in Bagneux from 1982 to 1988, when it was moved to a larger house in Champs sur Marne, yet another southeastern suburb of Paris. After all these splits, a centripetal tendency manifested itself: the monks of Rennes, Bordeaux, Marseilles, and Lyons formed a single Buddhist association and now cooperate closely.

These monasteries in resettlement countries differ from their Cambodian models in several ways. Visually, they occupy flats and suburban houses that are not differentiated in any way from the surrounding buildings. The only exceptions are probably the vast complex being built in Maryland in the United States, an actual Khmer temple being completed in Sydney, Australia, on grounds provided for a Cambodian community center, and the Wat Khemâraram temple at Créteil, which is built quite low and wider than long. The temple, invisible from the street, is somewhat reminiscent of Cambodian architecture.

As most of these institutions are located in residential houses, they do not have sufficient space for large gatherings during annual festivals, and supporters must hire community halls for these occasions. In Paris, such festivals always take place at the International Buddhist temple in the Bois de Vincennes. Because the three Parisian monasteries insist on celebrating these occasions separately, there are not only three Cambodian *kâthĕn* (ceremonies for presenting new robes to the monks) each year, but also three New Years's celebrations, and three feasts for ancestors, all on different weekends but in the same place.

Wherever it is economically feasible, Cambodians found their own monasteries, where they can communicate in Khmer and where all the symbols are familiar. There are a number of Khmer monasteries in the United States, Australia, and Europe. In addition, there were monasteries in the border settlements in Thailand, even in Khmer Rouge camps. In the west, in contrast to the situation in Cambodia, there are no monasteries situated in the center of cities; all are located in suburbs where land is cheaper, but convenient only for those supporters who live nearby. Where monasteries are not available, the Khmers may support any Theravada monks visiting on invitation, and in such countries as Britain, where there are relatively few Cambodians, Thai, Sinhalese, or western monks are invited to their ceremonies, although a Khmer monk is highly esteemed and made especially welcome. Of the fifty thousand Cambodians resident in France, about twenty thousand live in greater Paris, and of these the Sino-Khmers are concentrated mainly in the 13th, 18th, and 19th districts of the city, while the Khmers are scattered throughout the city and suburbs (Tan Yim Phong 1984). Yet all three Cambodian monasteries are located in the southeastern suburbs.

Administratively, the organization of monasteries in resettlement countries depends to some degree on the laws of the country. In France and probably in most western countries, these religious institutions are run by duly constituted charitable asso-

ciations with elected presidents, secretaries, and treasurers, and
with proper bookkeeping and audits. As many young Khmers
choose to study either computer programming or accounting, information is usually stored on a computer. For older Cambodians,
fixed membership fees are new and unusual, because in Cambodia
contributions from supporters were at least theoretically voluntary
and unspecified, although people certainly knew how much was
expected of them. Also in Cambodia, the committee managing
the monastery was composed of laymen separate from the monastic organization, although they often held meetings together.
In France, however, a monk is often president or secretary of the
association.

The difference between the organization if Khmer Buddhism at
the local level in Cambodia "before" and resettlement countries
now is most striking in another aspect. In Cambodia, where the
ruler was the protector of Buddhism, the community of monks was
organized in a hierarchy and supervised by the state. The hierar-
chization started at the bottom of the pyramid at the local level,
where every monastery had an abbot and two secretaries, all ap-
proved by the higher echelons of the *sângkh,* or organization of
Buddhist clergy. Each monastic district had a head monk called
ânŭkeănĕa, with a *mékon* at the head of every province. There
were district assemblies and provincial assemblies.

At the head of the monastic order were the supreme patriarch
(*Sânghanayaka,* who may have received the royal title *sângkhâreach*
from the king) and high dignitaries forming the monastic assembly
(Chau Seng 1962). These high ranks were conferred by royal de-
cree. Although these appointments were made on the recommen-
dation of the *sângkh,* the government had some right of selection
and the right of veto. Monks were expected to be overtly nonpo-
litical: they could not vote in a general election or be elected to
parliament. But they had political influence and used it, either as
advisers to politicians or as advisers to voters. The government
kept them under formal control by issuing to all monks identity
cards that had to be shown whenever required.

There was never any organization of all Theravada Buddhists,
and monks were normally organized into a national *sângkh.* In
Thailand, monks of both the Thommâyŭt and Mohanĭkay orders

are organized into a single hierarchy under one supreme patriarch; in Cambodia there was a hierarchy for each order, each with its own supreme patriarch at the top. With few exceptions (Ebihara 1966), Thommâyŭt institutions are limited to urban areas, while the Mohanĭkay has more followers spread throughout the country.

Thai or Sri Lankan monasteries located in the west remain in contact with monks in their country of origin; Thai appointments abroad are made in Bangkok, and Thai people come by air from Bangkok to present *kâthĕn* offerings to these monasteries. The ties of Cambodian refugees to their homeland, however, were cut off when Phnom Penh fell in 1975, and there is no overall Khmer Buddhist organization in resettlement countries, just individual monastic residences and associations. This system is, of course, very similar to the ancient system as described in the *Vinaya*. When the dying Buddha was asked who should succeed him, he said that the monks should be led by his teaching alone.

This latitude and lack of governmental influence seems ideal, but ambitious monks in exile miss the opportunity for social advancement. Venerable Buer Kry once showed me a fan with an embroidered inscription: "Head of all monks in France." It is not clear who gave it to him. Recently, he received the title *sâmtec ubâchcha* from Prince Sihanouk in recognition of his role as the preceptor of one of Sihanouk's sons when he was a temporary monk at Wat Khemâraram. This term differs, however, from *sâmtec prĕah sângkh neayŭak*, the supreme patriarch.

Venerable Buer Kry stresses differences in rank in various ways; for instance, during services within his temple he does not sit with other monks but at a right angle to them on a special seat with a backrest. When he was invited to Germany, he sent a number of monks and nuns to prepare the ceremony site before his arrival, and he himself traveled later by more comfortable transport. In addition, the Créteil monastery is said to charge high fees for ceremonies. This monastery is the richest monastery in Paris, and the only one with a temple delimited by boundary stones, which have been consecrated according to custom.

In Cambodia, most people supported the monastery nearest to their homes. In Phnom Penh, where there was a wide choice, people were able to use different monasteries for different purposes. I

knew one intellectual who frequented Wat Unnalôm (Vât Unnalôm), where he had friends among the scholarly monks. When he
fell sick and doctors were unable to help him, his wife insisted on
trying a healing ritual; in the end he agreed, but he did not want
his rational monastic friends to know about his lapse into "folk
superstition," and he called monks from the nearest monastery to
perform the ceremony. He soon recovered, but I am sure he never
mentioned this experience at Wat Unnalôm.

The criteria for choosing a monastery differs in Cambodia and
Paris. In France, the choice of monastery does not depend on geographical location, nor does a person use two monasteries for different needs. According to several informants, the choice depends
on ethnicity, class, political persuasion, and attitude to folk religion. Wat Khemâraram is supported by Prince Sihanouk and some
members of his family, by rich Sino-Khmers, and by people interested in horoscopes and healing rituals. Wat Bodhivansa is supported by Prince Sisowath Essaro and his part of the royal family,
by professional Khmers, and by people who scorn practices like
horoscopes. Followers of Son Sann also prefer this monastery. The
monastery at Bagneux is relatively recent, but it is said to attract
peasants and nonprofessional Khmers, some of whom are no
doubt attracted to the personality of the chief monk. These divisions are not clear-cut, but I met only one person who was a member both of the association connected to Wat Khemâraram and the
association connected to Wat Bodhivansa. Few people support
more than one monastery.

Money is collected in ways similar to those used in Cambodia.
In Prek Por (Preak Pô) (Cambodia), where I stayed for some time,
one of the lay committee members went to all the houses of the
locality every month or two with a copybook, into which each supporter inscribed the sum he was contributing. As everybody saw
what his neighbors gave, generosity was encouraged, but generally
the rates were established by tradition and depended on family
circumstances, averaging perhaps one hundred riels at a time. (In
the early 1960s, one hundred riels equaled one U.S. dollar; the
unofficial rate between 1959 and 1960 was seventy-five riels to
one U.S. dollar.) Separate amounts were sometimes collected for

special needs. The money was used for everyday expenditures for the monastery.

A silver bowl was also passed around the congregation during services, and everybody present contributed. In 1966, the usual amount was one riel in the village, five riel at major ceremonies at which the provincial head officiated, and ten riel at the *vât* (temple) of the supreme patriarch. This money went to the monk or monks involved in the ceremony. Although theoretically monks are not to handle gold or silver, meaning money, in practice banknotes were presented in an envelope so that monks would not have to touch them. If they needed to buy something, they sent a lay person to get it for them. Many monks received salaries; for instance, when they taught in any educational institution, they could have bank accounts and write checks.

Cambodian monasteries rarely owned land other than that on which they were built, but if they held fields that were let for cultivation, they could not enforce the payment of rent and might not get very much when they were able to collect. Any land presented to a monastery, however, was inalienable and could not be sold.

In Paris, some money is collected through membership subscriptions, but not enough to maintain the monastery. I had access only to the membership list of Wat Bodhivansa, where some three hundred members each paid three hundred francs a year in fees, although some of them contributed more; this probably would not have sufficed to maintain the monastery. People present not only food and transport at every service and ceremony, but cash as well. There are collection boxes at every shrine. During New Year celebrations and during *phchŭm bĕn* (Festival for the Dead) at Bois de Vincennes, several thousand Cambodians often congregate, and the collection may be substantial; it is also a matter of prestige to collect more than another monastery does on the same occasion. When a monastery needs large amounts of money for a new building, for example, it organizes a fund-raising ceremony, to which many outsiders are invited.

But in contrast to practices in prewar Cambodia, most of this money would not stay with the monastery; money was collected at these occasions primarily for refugees in Thailand. And soon after the rainy season, a group of monks and nuns traveled to Thailand to distribute this money. Although monks cannot handle money personally, the nuns can, and sending monastics has some advantage because Thai officers are bound to show some respect to Buddhist monks.

The women I refer to as nuns are not true nuns (*phĭkkhŭni*), as their line of ordination died out in Theravada countries centuries ago, but white-clad women observing the eight precepts and living mostly in monasteries where they meditate and also perform many useful chores. The same path is open to men, but few follow it, partly because traditionally only elderly lay people practiced their religion seriously, and as women usually survive men, more women were available for this option. Moreover, a man can become a monk, which earns him more merit as well as more respect. Women, whether nuns or not, can be influential but usually keep in the background. One Cambodian woman organized the invitation of Venerable Yos Huot to Australia, where he founded a monastery in Adelaide and stayed about two years before he joined the United Nations Border Relief Organization (UNBRO) in Thailand.[1]

The nuns at Wat Khemâraram are a group of friends who seem very happy, active, and partisan, collecting information about other monastic residences. When Wat Bodhivansa was still at Bagneux, a nun resident there had a special room built for herself in the garden. She was a very energetic organizer, and always traveled with monks to Thailand. She had been the wife of the monk from Rennes before he became ordained. When Wat Bodhivansa moved, she stayed on, and her former husband later took over the building as a branch of his Rennes monastery. He now commutes between the two.

One innovation that seems to be limited to Paris is the use of women as leaders of the congregation during services in the monastery. In Cambodia, this function was always performed by a man, usually somebody who had spent several years as a monk, and it was a very respected role. But in Paris, knowledgeable men are not always available on weekdays. Mrs. Hak Prou, one of the staunchest supporters of Wat Bodhivansa, had been a nun as a young girl in Cambodia, and later in Burma, where she studied

Pali. Still later, she disrobed and married. One day when the congregation at Wat Bodhivansa could not find any experienced man to lead them, she offered her services because she knew all the Pali formulas by heart. That substitution was merely an emergency measure, but the experiment was a success and since that time she has been asked to preside quite often. This must have been the inspiration for Wat Khemâraram to adopt the practice, and Venerable Buer Kry started teaching some of the nuns there the relevant Pali texts. I was present on one occasion when a nun led the congregation there, and she read the text, but the nuns will no doubt memorize texts given sufficient time. This improved status of women in Buddhist temples is, however, not welcomed by everyone, and some supporters at the temple in Bagneux have criticized this development.

Although old people in France still use the temples in the traditional ways (Kalab 1990), young men show little interest in becoming monks. This trend was already apparent in prewar urban Cambodia. Some do not like to spend their office leave in a monastery, or to explain to their French friends afterward why they shaved their heads. French-educated Cambodians who are interested in Buddhism often have western attitudes toward it: they are willing to study the philosophy and meditation but shun the rituals. A young man may retain this attitude even when he does become a monk. The son of one important supporter of Venerable Buer Kry became ordained at Wat Khemâraram, and for much of the time was the only person there who spoke fluent French. From the start, he was interested more in meditation and books on eastern philosophy than in learning to calculate horoscopes from Venerable Buer Kry. He is now in charge of a branch of Wat Khemâraram in Brussels.

When I visited the location, a nun from Wat Khemâraram was looking after him, and a number of Belgians frequented his meditation classes. He meditated virtually the entire day, and tried to move from his city house to a farm near Brussels where there would be quieter, natural surroundings. But the Cambodians in Belgium reportedly were not very happy with this genuine young monk, because they preferred someone keen on organizing large festivals and officiating at innumerable domestic ceremonies.

In this case, the young man's predilection for the contemplative life was inspired by French books. But there have always been monks in Cambodia who lived in forests or meditation *asramas* and were greatly respected by the population. In addition, there were some scholars in Phnom Penh who scorned rituals, and monks of this persuasion were found even in villages among those who knew no western language. But there were always enough other monks who were happy to perform any number of ceremonies desired by their supporters. In the smaller Buddhist populations in the west, not everyone can be accommodated.

The relation between monk and layman in Paris differs slightly from that in Cambodia. There, it was best expressed during the daily almsround. The monk stands with his bowl, barefoot, eyes downcast, in front of the house, asking for nothing. The lay person approaches him, greets him respectfully, and spoons some rice into his bowl. The lay person gives this nourishment to the monk in order to acquire merit. But in Paris, Cambodians live scattered throughout the city, and the prospect of walking barefoot in the winter in snow prevents traditional almsrounds. In practice, therefore, every monastery is looked after by a lay person or nun who does the cooking on days when the monks are not invited to a ceremony and when no supporter has promised to bring food. As monks may eat only food presented to them, some lay person is essential to perform this task.

Also in Cambodia, although monks received the utmost respect from lay people, they were also disciplined by layfolk. Villagers had their own ways of disciplining monks informally. Once a monk came from another hamlet to see me without having been specifically invited. This was deemed wrong. My landlady prostrated herself before him but ignored his thirst and refused to provide tea. This denial would probably not have happened in the anonymity of urban society with its different customs.

Buddhist rituals follow the lunar calendar, and each monastery in Paris prints an annual calendar in which the lunar months are superimposed on the solar ones. Primary western holidays are indicated, as well as all full-moon days, new-moon days, and the eighth day following each of these, and all are marked as days of precepts, just as they used to be on the official monastic calendar in Cambodia. All other important Buddhist dates are also indicated, such as entry into the rainy season retreat, the end of the rainy season, *vĭsakh bauchea* (the festival at the end of the rainy season), and the fortnight of *bĕn* (the period leading up to the festival of the dead). If there is sufficient planning and all the dates are known in January, the days of the main festivals at Bois de Vincennes, including *kâthĕn,* are indicated as well.

The services duplicate those held in Cambodia as much as possible. Recitations there were standardized by the issuing of official books of texts: one for monks, another for laymen.[2] In addition, Radio Phnom Penh started every day with a religious service broadcast from one of three Phnom Penh monasteries where laymen were trained for precision in the chanting of Buddhist liturgy. These services were Mohanĭkay or Thommâyŭt versions on alternate days. In Paris, recitations still follow the same books. In Cambodia, services on the days of precepts were normally attended only by a few old people who asked for them, with attendance increasing during the rainy season. In contrast, large festivals may attract several thousand to these services in Paris.

These festivals are also occasions for conspicuous competition, as people feel free to come to the feast at Bois de Vincennes so that they can compare the performances of Cambodian musicians and singers, the standard of folk dances, the special show put on by the Cambodian royal ballet, and the wit of the folk singers. They also compare the food provided at lunchtime and the overall organization. Above all, they want to know how much money was collected on each occasion. These are also opportunities to meet friends, often unexpected visitors from abroad, and to buy from shopkeepers selling Cambodian textiles, pictures, books, and food.

Phchŭm bĕn is a more solemn occasion without afternoon entertainment, and its observance differs somewhat from what I observed in Cambodia, although there were variations in the Brahmanic portion of the service in the homeland as well. The fortnight of offerings to ancestors begins on the first day of the waning moon during the month of *photrobât* [September-October]. Every day at Prek Por, between three and four in the morning, drumming from the temple called people to the dawn service, during which riceballs were offered to the ancestors, one ball on the first day, two on the second, and so on. After the service, the offerings were thrown to the dogs outside near a spirit shrine. During this service, the monks always chanted the *Parabhava Sutta* [the sixth *sutta* of the *Sutta Nipata* (Chalmers 1932)], which was also chanted daily on the radio during these fifteen days.

After a few hours of rest, there followed the morning service and lunch. In the evening there was a sermon. On the last day, people brought enormous quantities of Cambodian cakes wrapped in banana leaves to the temple, and most families had *bângsŏlkaul* performed for their ancestors. (*Bângsŏlkaul* [commonly pronounced *bângskaul*] is a ceremony in which four monks recite texts while connected by a white cord to an urn containing ashes of ancestors. In this way, merit is transferred to the departed. It is a time of exodus to native villages in Cambodia, to the places where these ashes are kept.)

In Paris, *phchŭm bên* services are simplified, and although there may be daily services in the monasteries, dawn services rarely, if ever, occur. At Créteil this omission is justified by fear that the gong would disturb French neighbors. Riceballs are not offered at ceremonies. In addition, *Parabhava Sutta* is not recited; surprisingly, this *sutta* was never included in the book for monks despite its regular use in Cambodia, probably because this book may have been copied in Thailand, where important feasts for the ancestors are not held. *Bângsŏlkaul* ceremonies also cannot be performed exactly in the traditional way because the ashes of ancestors are back in Cambodia and those who perished during the Pol Pot regime were not even cremated. During the collective ritual for the dead in Bois de Vincennes, people usually write down the names of their dead relatives on a sheet of paper, which circulates among the congregation, to make sure that they will be included in the merit sharing. The paper is then burned during the ritual, a custom thought to be of Chinese origin. Finally, in contrast to Cambodian practice, the Parisian congregation never asks for the Eight Precepts, straying from normal procedures at the morning services during the important festivals in the homeland.

In the homeland, very old monks or less-educated ones who were not good speakers always read their sermons from palm leaf manuscripts or books. Young educated monks tended to be good orators and often spoke without notes, using examples from everyday life in the village in ordinary spoken language. Their sermons were far more popular; although old ladies sat through any sermon, even when they were sleepy and did not understand much, because hearing the sermon was meritorious. In Paris, no one reads a sermons.

Monks perform tasks that are not strictly religious. Educating is one of their more traditional activities, and as there are no Cambodian schools in Paris, children who wish to learn to read and write Khmer attend weekend classes run by various groups of volunteers. Venerable Sar Sastr is one of the teachers. At Wat Khemâraram, one monk is an expert carpenter and produces preaching chairs in the traditional style. Another monk makes statues of the Buddha in various sizes, which are sold to the followers. Another traditional art is reading horoscopes, as Venerable Buer Kry does. Other aspects of Khmer folk religion may be observed at this monastery, which is where Ang Chouléan collected much of his information on folk religion (1980, 1982, 1986, 1988). The monks are ready to experiment with any traditional craft. For example, they attempted to cut, stitch, and dye several *kâthĕn* robes within the specified time limit even though every monk, including those in Asia, relies on receiving ready-made robes nowadays. While seemingly limited in scope and significance, these efforts may constitute an important avenue for the monks to maintain some aspects of their traditional culture.

A more controversial activity of the monks, is the shift toward more political involvement. In Thailand, the government's use of monks to organize development projects is being criticized as being inappropriate to their traditional role. In Cambodia, however, the secretary of the monastery of one village organized the construction of a medical center without such criticism. The difference seems to be the source of the projects' initiation and motivation: governmental in Thailand, from the monks themselves in Cambodia. The Heng Samrin (PRK) government in Cambodia certainly tries to indoctrinate monks in their political views in the hope that they will spread them, but this is the extent of the monks' political involvement. In Paris, however, the Venerable Buer Kry reportedly asked supporters to contribute money to Sihanouk's

army, contradicting the tradition that monks have nothing to do
with war. Son Sann established a Khmer Buddhist Research Center
at Rithisen and contributed to its first publication (1986:157):

> Part of this grand strategy of renaissance of Buddhism in Cambodia
> is our awareness that the monks cannot remain in their monasteries
> and wait until the people go visit them and ask for their help. Now
> the monks have been actively leaving their monasteries and have
> gone to the people, asking after their daily material and spiritual
> needs, offering help, and advising them about the difficulties they
> face. The monks have also expanded their knowledge in political
> and social questions and started to exercise influence in regard to
> motivating the population for the liberation of their country from
> foreign domination and the Marxist-Leninist ideology.

At a temporary Khmer village belonging to Son Sann's group on
the border of Buriram in Thailand, the leader told me that when
Heng Samrin's soldiers desert and wish to join Son Sann's army,
they are first ordained monks and for several weeks are taught traditional values and morality.

This change is not paralleled in Paris, where the monks continue
to remain independent of politics, although monks everywhere are
concerned for their homeland. Politicians wish to use the *sângkh*
because monks are trusted by the people. But they will be trusted
only as long as they stay independent of any government and are
free to express their own opinions on such ethical problems as corruption. A tamed *sângkh* will not be of any use to anyone.

Meanwhile, the monasteries in Paris lead their separate lives and
compete with one another for prestige and number of supporters.
In addition to competition over the size of collections and the standard of entertainment at festivals, they also seem to value contact
with outsiders. One is told how many English or Japanese monks
visited Wat Bodhivansa, and Bagneux is proud of its close connection with Venerable Maha Ghosananda, who is involved in a peace
movement in the United States. Wat Khemâraram is said to have
organized a *bângsŏlkaul* for the late Bernard Groslier, a French ar-
chaeologist, to which prominent French academics were invited.

But all these activities are viewed as possibly temporary, while
hope for a free, independent and democratic Cambodia endures.

Most of the differences between prewar Cambodian Buddhist practices and current overseas practices are superficial and easily reversible—woolen pullovers, stockings, and coats with hoods depend only on climate. The lack of special seats for monks on public transport means that some always wait for a car or taxi, while others brave the Metro and take the risk that a woman may touch them.

The followers remain prepared to sacrifice much for their monastery because they believe it is an essential institution. Should the situation last several decades, however, it is not certain that today's teenagers will feel the same need for traditional Buddhist practices as their parents do while growing old. The recruitment of monks is also precarious, and those who are recruited cannot attend traditional Pali schools, as there are none.

Many manuscripts were destroyed during the war. Almost all the old well-educated and experienced monks are dead, so that oral tradition is limited as well. Despite all these handicaps and the influences of foreign cultures, Cambodian Buddhism is surviving in Paris in its several forms and in both orders. Although the *sângkh* has no central organization and is far from united, the competitive spirit among individual institutions brings its own discipline as each temple wishes to prove its own good qualities. Experiences gained in foreign countries may prove useful in the long run, and Cambodia may benefit in the future from a worldwide independent *sângkh*.

CHAPTER SIX

Khmer Buddhists in the United States: Ultimate Questions

Carol A. Mortland

A primary challenge to traditional Khmer Buddhism in the United States is to explain the events that have occurred in Cambodia in the past two or three decades, most especially, finding explanations for the years when the country was ruled by the Khmer Rouge. For Khmer Buddhists, when ordinary conditions do not respond to physical or propitiatory measures, the lack of a solution can be attributed to error in specific human action. When extraordinary events occur, however, the very essence of a social group's otherworldly explanations becomes problematic. So while Khmer have for centuries utilized karmic theory to explain unusual or threatening events, the Democratic Kampuchea years were of such extraordinary horror that usual explanations for the extraordinary did not always suffice. This chapter explores Khmer description and explanation and the implications that acts committed during the Khmer Rouge years have for Khmer refugees.

For the 150,000 Khmer who have arrived in the United States since the late 1970s, the Pol Pot era and the experience of concentration camp life (which is, in effect, what life in Cambodia became between 1975 and 1979), flight, and refugee camps are virtually inexplicable.[1] I mean the term "inexplicable" to indicate a type of response among Khmer to vital questions and the chimera of answers—the sense of events overwhelming an individual or group, the sense that traditional ways of conceptualizing answers to such events are no longer suitable but lead to confusion and anxiety. Answers to the inexplicable do not have the force and permanence of earlier answers: the issues return, the questions do not rest, the answers are insufficient, and additional ones need to be piled on.

The questions Khmer are trying to ask include: Why did these events occur in Cambodia to Khmer? How are Khmer to deal with them? How do we Khmer explain them? How do we live with the enormous changes that have occurred in our homeland and have forced us to live under drastically different conditions? These questions have to do not only with Cambodians' ultimate questions but with their everyday lives: when a Cambodian refugee in San Diego asks why he has survived, he is asking a question that is certainly concerned with the most solemn, more ultimate questions humans ask, but that also has bearing on his everyday life—how he is to live it, endure it (see Leach 1968; Tambiah 1970; Myerhoff 1978; Bateson and Bateson 1987; Gombrich and Obeyesekere 1988 for discussions on ultimate questions).

Alternate Explanations

How do Cambodians' ultimate questions present difficulties for them in the new world? Their questions do not go away. Again and again, Khmer ask themselves and others what one Khmer man asks about the loss of his wife and son during Pol Pot times: "Was Any's disappearance some sort of punishment on us both for leaving Nawath? Or my punishment for allowing her to come with me? Did Any's death somehow ensure my survival? Because there are no answers, the questions haunt me still, and always will" (Yathay 1987:238).

In over ten years of talking with Khmer refugees in a multitude of settings, I have listened to hundreds of Cambodians describe what happened to them and ask why. Cambodians must reassess ultimate answers because traditional answers are unsatisfactory. Both the questioning and the inadequacy of traditional answers leads to Khmers' identity begin shaken: a young Khmer writes that during Pol Pot times "we were not humans." This Khmer student says that people become like zombies, "hardly recognizing one another." In the face of this inhumanity—not feeling oneself as human, not perceiving others as human—"I could only plead, 'Oh God! What is the purpose of life?'" (Kchao 1989:12).

These questions also haunt those Khmer who did not live in Democratic Kampuchea. Cynthia M. Coleman, describing Khmer living in the United States during the Pol Pot period, claims that they have experienced a depression "which few people in the world—except holocaust victims and victims of massive natural disasters—had ever experienced: the sense of inexplicably having survived" (1987:366). Coleman continues: "Some Cambodians, although not many, had turned away from Buddhism in anger and despair, saying that Buddhism was to blame for what had happened to their beloved Cambodia. Perhaps the Christian God, working through the church groups trying to help them, was a better choice. . . . The few who became Christian for the most part did so because they were searching for answers to unthinkable questions" (1987:366). There are two issues to explore here: first, how do Cambodians *explain* what has occurred to them? Second, how do they *react* to what has occurred to them?

The explanations of ordinary Khmer for extraordinary events begin with description: individual descriptions of what happened to oneself, generalized descriptions of what occurred to Cambodians during the Khmer Rouge years, and descriptions of cause. The first are framed in "this occurred to *me*" statements; the second in "this is what happened to *us*" assertions, and the third in "this is who *did* it to us" statements: "The Khmer Rouge did . . . to us." One American researcher, knowledgeable about Cambodian resettlement realities and reactions, claims that Khmer refugees have been trying to integrate their experiences with interpretation since resettlement began after 1979, but have not yet achieved such integration or evolved a collective interpretation of the Khmer Rouge period (Mollica 1987).

Christianity and Khmer Refugees

A likely reaction of Khmer refugees to the changes that have occurred to them and their systems of belief and behavior would be to explore an alternate religion. Anne R. Hansen and Bounthay Phath hypothesized that because Buddhism might not "provide a concrete enough interpretation of [Cambodians'] individual and collective experiences of trauma," they might turn to Christianity (1987:15). There is some evidence for this view. Michael Vickery (1984:12) saw "massive" disaffection among Khmer in Thai refugee camps, where there were more registered Christians in 1980 than in the entire country of Cambodia before 1970.[2] Some observers saw the conversion of Khmer Buddhists in the refugee camps to Christianity as resulting from proselytizing among a vulnerable population by foreign missionaries. But Vickery claims that to accuse missionaries of creating Khmer "rice Christians" is off the mark, and he quotes Khmer acquaintances who said, "'Look at what happened to Cambodia under Buddhism; Buddhism has failed, and we must search for some other faith'" (12).

Bounthan is an example of a Khmer who has chosen a new religion for her answers and religious practices. She has been in America almost ten years and is now a practicing Christian.[3] She fled to Thailand in 1979, where she was eventually placed in a refugee camp. Here, in relative safety, receiving rations of food, water, and fuel, she contemplated what had happened to her and why. And it was here that she had the experience that changed her religious commitment. One night she had a dream about a church. "I didn't know about church. I saw the lady with long white clothes. I asked her, 'Can I go across the river?'[4] She talked to me, but I don't remember what she said. After that I woke up. I wanted to go to church, but I didn't know where to go." Bounthan told a foreigner of her dream, and the woman took her to church.

From that time, Bounthan decided "to believe in Jesus." She went to church every morning from five-thirty to seven-thirty, and studied the Bible with the minister from nine to eleven. She began to learn to read Khmer so that she could read the Bible in her own language. She did not have relatives in the United States but was accepted for resettlement here, and thus is convinced that God helped her obtain refugee status and resettlement in America. As she was transferred to other processing centers on her way to the United States, she prayed to God when she was frightened—during subsequent interviews in processing centers, in strange airports

and while traveling on airplanes, when feeling physically ill, and
when arriving in a new place.

Bounthan says some Khmer became Christians because "people
said you go faster to America if you become a Christian," but she
is adamant that this is not the reason she became a Christian: "I
did not know about Jesus before my dream. I did not know about
church before my dream" (see Ashe 1988). Bounthan does not
know what kind of Christianity she studied in the refugee camp.
Since coming to the United States, she has attended her sponsors'
churches, Methodist and Presbyterian, which she says are just
like the services she attended in the Thai refugee camp and the
Philippine processing center. When asked what Christians believe,
Bounthan replied, "They believe the Bible. They believe Jesus."
Although there are Khmer refugees who, like Bounthan, have become Christians and no longer consider themselves Buddhists,
many who are interested in Christianity express continued interest
in Buddhism and consider themselves Buddhists.

A major issue for Khmer is whether a person can be both Buddhist and Christian. Although Khmer differ as to whether a person
can be both, Judy Ledgerwood (1990b) suggests that most Khmer
see the two world views as compatible, that they now accept that
both belief systems can be practiced by the same person, and that
they utilize both systems for description and explanation of past
and present reality. Some Khmer recognize that most American
Christians do not accept that Christians can be Buddhists at the
same time, while other Khmer say Americans do accept that both
belief systems can be practiced by the same person.

Whether or not Americans—especially those with whom
Khmer are in contact—accept Khmer conversion to Christianity is
vitally important to Khmer for a number of reasons. First, Christianity as an alternate belief system holds much of its attraction for
Khmer because it is followed by what they perceive to be people
more powerful than themselves. Thus it may offer more advantages and perhaps more protection for Khmer than does Buddhism. Second, many Khmer believe that survival and advancement in America requires some degree of assimilation to American
ways: since many Americans are Christians, Khmer in America
should also be Christians. Third, Khmer are eager to please the

Americans who have assisted them the most: many of these Americans are Christians, and Khmer believe that an acceptance of Christian ritual and belief is an act of gratitude to caring and more powerful Americans.

Finding Answers in Khmer Buddhism

Most Khmer refugees in the United States, however, do not become Christians but seek answers in the practice of traditional Khmer Buddhism in America. Khmer refugees have spent considerable time and energy in gathering together or re-creating the environment that makes such practice possible.

The collective practice of traditional Khmer Buddhism in the United States was rare before 1979; since then, more than fifty Khmer temples have been established in communities throughout the country. It is at these temples that many of the Khmer refugees now regularly practice Cambodian Buddhist rites. Where no temples exist, Khmer observe their religious rituals in homes and community halls on an irregular basis. As there were fewer than two hundred Khmer and only three Khmer temples in the United States in 1979 (Coleman 1987) before the flight of hundreds of thousands of Khmer from their homeland and their resettlement abroad, this is a phenomenon of rapid religious change.

The restoration of Buddhism for Khmer refugees who have resettled in the United States is expressed primarily through aspects of Buddhism which are public and which center on the temple. These include holding merit-making festivals, conducting religious healings, and building and supporting temples.[5] Very important, the restoration also occurs through the observation of Buddhist festivals: for example, New Year, and *phchŭm bĕn* (the Festival for the Dead).

The Khmer perceive merit-making activities performed by individuals, such as contributing food and money to a temple and attending Buddhist ceremonies, and individual "right behavior" as essential for maintaining natural and social order. One's acts affect the quality and quantity of harvests, hierarchical relationships, and, in fact the "cyclical flow of the cosmic order" (Smith 1989:

13; see Ebihara 1966; Thierry 1985). Frank Smith adds, "Just how essential the maintenance of this order is becomes apparent when one considers the perceived consequences of a break in that order—such as Khmer Rouge rule and the subsequent desecration of Buddhist temples and defrocking of monks" (1989:13). It is thus vitally important that necessary structures be reestablished in order that Cambodians can again practice the rituals that help ensure order in their world.

Interestingly, Christian communities in America are supporting the reestablishment of Khmer Buddhism. For example, a Christian church in Massachusetts provided space for a substitute village temple that offered Buddhist ceremonies, weddings, and study groups, and its church members gave technical assistance for organizing large Khmer ceremonies (Hansen 1988). A Lutheran church in Pennsylvania regularly provided worship space for an itinerant Khmer Buddhist monk, and another Protestant church in New York gave one thousand dollars to assist local Khmer refugees in sponsoring a monk from a refugee camp in Thailand.

Yet Christianity continues to be perceived by the majority of Khmer refugees as a threat to Khmer Buddhism in the United States. I was told by numerous Khmer in various cities that Christians, who were kind to Cambodians and helped them find jobs, were among the greatest threats to Khmer Buddhism in the United States because they made Cambodians think about becoming Christians. A monk in a large midwestern city said, "Khmer Buddhism can help these refugees sitting here, but we cannot survive in the future because there are so many Christians in America."

For Khmer who continue to frame their world view and ultimate questions in terms of Cambodian Buddhism, the questions that arise and the answers that emerge because of the recent tragedy of their country and lives fall into several distinct sets. I turn to these now.

Suffering and Individual Responsibility

One answer given by Khmer to explain the Pol Pot years is to say that to be born is to suffer, to live is to suffer. For many Khmer, suffering is the first step to understanding what has occurred to them; this understanding is then followed by an inquiry into cause and effect.

Khmer Buddhists believe in *kâm:* that human action has consequences. This karmatic law, basic to Buddhist doctrine, states that each individual has free will and can act in a virtuous or an evil way; in addition, the universe operates according to a law by which virtue is rewarded and evil is punished, whether in this, a previous, or subsequent life (on defining Khmer Buddhism, see Porée-Maspero 1962–69; Thierry 1964, 1985; Ebihara 1966; Spiro 1967, 1970; Tambiah 1970, 1976; Kirsch 1981; and Ang Chouléan 1988, 1986). Acts committed in previous lives affect one's situation in this life and acts committed in this life will affect one's situation in a future life.

Thus, karmic law dictates that good action results in good, what Khmer Buddhists call *bŏn,* or merit. *Bŏn* can be a characteristic of a person or acquired by an individual for oneself or another person. Because *bŏn* comes from both "being" and "doing," it can be achieved both by being good or meritorious and by doing deliberate acts that increase *bŏn,* or merit, such as contributing money, time, or property to a temple. The acquisition of merit yields success—ability, money, good fortune—in other words, conditions and possessions that decrease suffering and increase contentment.

Just as karmic law dictates that the consequences of good action result in good for humans, so the consequences of bad action result in human suffering. Suffering is a central notion for Khmer Buddhists, and is caused when one does not follow Buddhist teaching. Thus when others cause pain, they are following the dictates of a cosmic fate. Khmer Buddhists view suffering as inevitable, and thus, in this view, there is no happiness without suffering.

Here is one Khmer Buddhist's explanation for what occurred in Cambodia in the 1970s, an explanation rooted in the belief in Cambodian proper order but concluding in the assumption of individual responsibility:

If your family is happy, you will have a good life. If all the families are happy, then the village will be happy. If all the villages are happy, then the land will be strong and content. . . .

I believed what the old monk taught me. And everything he said came true, only in reverse. My family was unhappy, my village was unhappy, and so was the country. And now I look back at it all and think about the connections, and wonder whether I myself was partly to blame (Ngor 1987:20).

Throughout the Khmer Rouge period, he and his wife "couldn't help wondering: Was there something in our past existence, some terrible deeds we had committed, that caused us to be punished by this regime?" Ngor Haing says that "plenty of Cambodians thought so, but they tended to be people who belonged to rather mystical and superstitious sects of Buddhism" (1987:157). Yet he and other less mystically oriented Buddhists often asked the same question, and posed the same answer.

Suffering and Collective Responsibility

Not only do Khmer question whether they themselves individually had done something terrible in the past to cause their suffering, they also wonder whether they, as a collectivity, were responsible for the suffering that occurred under Pol Pot. François Ponchaud (1989: 175) quotes a Khmer widow, of whose twelve children only three have survived: "I do not hate the Pol Pot regime. Such was our karma." This woman is clearly linking her suffering to collective Khmer karma, and she echoes what I have heard repeatedly in one form or another from Khmer: we Khmer have inflicted this upon ourselves.

In the collective view, however, most Khmer refugees do not usually see the infliction as having been caused by their own actions, but by other Khmer, to whom they are joined in a collectivity. Many Khmer agree with a monk who said that the "Khmer Rouge regime forced many people to suffer, but this was the result of the previous regime's policies that had also caused so much suffering." In this view, the Pol Pot years continued the *bap* that began when Sihanouk was toppled from power and a middle path of neutrality and balance was abandoned. "From 1970 onward, the cause and the effect of suffering was more suffering" (Hansen and Phath 1987:31, 32). A young Khmer university student also asks this larger question: "Could it be possible that my beloved sister Tevdara and millions of others were victims of Sihanouk as well as victims of the Khmer Rouge?" (Kchao 1989:13).

Thus, in the Khmer view, people higher in the social hierarchy can cause suffering to innocent people who are lower. In Khmer culture, the acts of one person can dishonor the entire family and bring suffering in their wake, not just for the individual but for others. Here we have a dialectic with hierarchy: the high can bring suffering to the low. Similarly, the low can bring suffering to the high, through such acts as disrespect, betrayal, or deception.

Ngor suggests that some Khmer where willing to submit to the Khmer Rouge "as if surrendering to their fates," but he did not agree with them: "To me, whether we had good *kâm* or bad *kâm*, it was important to fight the Khmer Rouge" (1987:157). Thus, while many refugees use their collective unfortunate karma to explain the Pol Pot terrors and their own complete submission and powerlessness during that era, Ngor claims that action is possible, even necessary, against fate.

Another Khmer, a university-educated Buddhist and Ngor's friend, exhibits a larger context for questioning: "It is easy to blame it all on *kâm*, but the fact is that real world events made this new regime. . . . If we are being punished for anything, it is that we have abandoned the middle way" (quoted in Ngor 1987:158). For this resettled refugee, comprehension of Pol Pot times does not refer to karma as much as to another vital Buddhist concept: that of balance, of remaining centered, within the middle way.

Predictions as Explanation

Many Khmer explain the Democratic Kampuchea period by reference to ancient Khmer prophecies. For example, Ngor claims that Khmer during Pol Pot times "believed that old prophecies were coming true and that Cambodia was being punished for sins committed long ago" (1987:157). These prophecies, translations of Pali scriptures that Khmer call *Pŭtth tŭmneay*, are predictions of supernatural signs of doom, including the ruin of Buddhism, which have a long history in the religious traditions of various Southeast Asian countries (Coedès 1956; Ishii 1976; Keyes

1977). Sam-Ang Sam says, "It was predicted in the Buddhist writing, the *Pŭtth tŭmneay,* Buddhism would be destroyed and it would be the end of our world, and what the *Pŭtth tŭmneay* said would happen happened—everything" (quoted in Florentine Films 1991:15). Numerous writers cite attempts by Khmer to place the Democratic Kampuchea period within the context of the *Pŭtth tŭmneay* (e.g., May Someth 1986; Szymusiak 1986).

Frank Smith (1989) says that Khmer familiar with these prophecies claim that they came to pass between 1970 and 1979. In fact, the prophecies were discussed in Phnom Penh in the early 1970s, even before the Khmer Rouge period (Schanberg 1972; Shawcross 1979; Hickey 1982; Becker 1986; Yathay 1987). Even those unfamiliar with the prophecies, when learning of the *Pŭtth tŭmneay,* are convinced of their applicability to the Khmer Rouge period; Smith quotes a young Khmer who first heard of the prophecies in the Thai refugee camps: "When I heard those predictions and then I compared them with the Khmer Rouge era, I was amazed... everything was predicted *exactly;* it wasn't just 'close.' 'The roads will be emptied of travellers, the houses will be emptied of people;'... 'the blood will flow in the streets as high as an elephant's stomach;'...'the worthless drunkards...will rise up to be great.' I saw all this happen myself, with my own eyes!" (1989:23).

According to the prophecies, this final period would be preceded by supernatural signs of the coming downfall, including the rusting of the sacred sword of Cambodia, the appearance of a comet, and the sighting of a white crocodile, a familiar symbol of doom in Khmer cosmology. In addition to describing the end as an era characterized by the suppression of Buddhism and much killing, other predictions are commonly cited by Khmer: the uneducated will rise to power, houses and streets will be emptied after a social and ecological catastrophe, and Buddhists will be persecuted by atheistic "enemies of the religion," or *tamĭl* (see Bizot 1976, 1980, 1981; Keyes and Daniel 1983).[6]

This is a description of the Cambodian prophecy by a Khmer refugee: "Puth [Pŭtth] was a nineteenth century sage who prophesied that the country would undergo a total reversal of traditional values. . . . But people would be saved if they planted the kapok tree—*kor,* in Cambodian. *Ko* also means 'mute.' The usual interpretation of this enigmatic message was that only the deaf-mutes would be saved during this period of calamity. . . . Therein, I now realized, lay the means of survival. Pretend to be deaf and dumb! Say nothing, hear nothing, understand nothing!" (Yathay 1987:63)[7]

Yathay Pin and his fellow countrymen increasingly believed in Pŭtth's predictions (Yathay 1987). Pŭtth had said that black crows would scatter *lvea* fruit throughout the land.[8] The *lvea* fruit is green, spherical, and shiny, apparently good to eat, but when opened it is filled with lice. Many Cambodian refugees tell how they viewed the Khmer Rouge cadres as the black crows, the *lvea* fruit as the utopian ideas of communism, and the lice as the contents of that ideology which were, in reality, killing, famine, and misery.

Pŭtth had said that, at the end, people will be so hungry they will chase a dog to fight over a grain of rice stuck to its tail. Yathay says that before 1975 "nobody believed in these predictions. When the elders talked about them, we would sneer and tease them. Who could imagine that famine would befall a country that exported rice? . . . Who would believe that of such a peaceful, unified country? Now, those terrible predictions were becoming truer every day. All values had been reserved and desecrators reigned" (1987:105, 106). For Yathay and his wife, their only occupation was survival, their only hope the predictions of Pŭtth, on whose words they depended: "Salvation comes from the West, and when peace reigns again, after the disappearance of the *tamĭl,* a new era will begin" (148).

Khmer refugees use these prophecies to explain Cambodia's continued economic distress. Smith's (1989:19–23) informants, for example, claim that the drought in Cambodia since 1979 has been the result of sacrilege by Pol Pot soldiers who, among other things, defrocked monks and destroyed temples and monuments.

Stories and Folklore as Explanation

Other Khmer continue to use traditional Cambodian stories that contain references to the law of karma to explain Pol Pot, just as they used them previously to explain the "inexplicable" (Ang Chouléan 1986). Smith (1989) claims that Khmer refugees also use folk tales to set the Khmer Rouge period within an understandable reality, for example the folk tale of the *kaun lôk* bird.[9] One of Smith's informants, describing how this bird abandoned her children in the forest so that they had to forage for food, compares this tale to the way the Khmer Rouge let the people starve so that they had to forage for food. Smith says that by drawing this conclusion his informant embeds his own Khmer Rouge experiences in a "larger historical and cosmic order" (24, 25).

Additional Explanations

Smith suggests that in addition to explanation through prophecy, legends, and folk tales, Khmer use two other means to explain the Khmer Rouge period. One deals with the notion of the Khmer Rouge as "uncivilized" and as participants in a specific Khmer tradition of violence and mythical existence; the second are accounts that focus on the role of Vietnam in the rise to power and the very nature of the Khmer Rouge. Thus Smith's informants link Khmer Rouge barbarism with descriptions of magical and historical acts, with spirits, animals, and evils of old. For example, Khmer Rouge soldiers ate human livers, a time-honored Cambodian ritual practiced at particular times.

Another Khmer refugee expresses dismay over the fact that the Khmer Rouge were indeed Khmer: "The hardest thing for me to explain, and the one thing that has broken my heart and troubled my spirit so, is that Pol Pot is a Khmer, just like me! Those [Khmer Rouge] soldiers were all Khmers, and they killed so many other Khmers. I don't know why" (Smith 1989:46). Some Khmer deal with this issue by denying that the tragedy of the 1970s was caused by Khmer (see also Ponchaud 1978; Ieng Mouly 1986). For example, some of Smith's informants exclaimed, on seeing Pol Pot's photograph for the first time, "He's not Khmer! He looks Chinese to me!" (1989:34). By suggesting that the Khmer Rouge period was created by outsiders, non-Khmer, by explaining it through prophecy, story, or history, Khmer place themselves in Khmer history and explain their experiences under Pol Pot.

Even the evil of the Khmer Rouge must be grounded in Khmer order. As individual experience under Pol Pot is embedded in Khmer history and social order by the retelling and linking of personal experience and traditional prophecy, story, and folk tale, "the 'story of Pol Pot,' with all its antecedents, descriptions and, to an extent, solutions, is firmly embedded in familiar 'reality'" (Smith 1989:43). To the extent that it is possible, the evil of Pol Pot becomes knowable in relation to Khmer history and context.

The problem remains that known context and "familiar reality" cannot sufficiently explain the atrocities of the Democratic Kampuchea period. Whether Khmer Buddhists convert to Christianity, take on the rituals of Christianity while continuing to believe in and practice Buddhism, or continue to view themselves as traditional Khmer Buddhists and only that, the struggle to find explanations and to answer ultimate questions is fierce. So, the experiences of Pol Pot, refugee life, and resettlement are compounded by the difficulty of explanation.

Answers That Do Not Satisfy

In describing the problem of interpreting Pol Pot, a young Khmer woman says, "There is a human tendency to believe that nothing really bad can happen to you—to the other person, perhaps, but not to you and your family, particularly when you've done nothing wrong" (Hansen and Phath 1987:150). Several Khmer agreed in Hansen's presence that they survived the Khmer Rouge period because they had done no evil. But during the same conversation, another Khmer said, "I am listening, and I respect your words, but still, I cannot comprehend why the three million were killed" (1987:21–22). Phath herself asks the ultimate question: "Now look at the holocaust in Cambodia. Why did the communists kill people? Most of the people were obedient to the *dharma*. Especially babies who were just born; why did communists throw them against the rock to shatter their skulls? Most

Cambodians say 'because we had bad karma.' But we have to ask
questions about this understanding. How could three million
people have bad karma at the same time?" (Hansen and Phath
1987:10).

She demonstrates her own doubt and suggests that of her fel-
lows when she states, Cambodians "are used to the law of karma;
but it doesn't always make sense" (1987:22). So for Phath, karma
may not account for holocaust; or it may, but then it also requires
additional exegesis. This is a vital point, if one is to understand at
all the daily conditions under which Khmer immigrants think and
feel about their lives.

When Cambodians question the law of karma, "they are questioning the most central aspect in Khmer Buddhism" (Hansen and
Phath 1987:22), thus bringing questions about the very legitimacy
of Khmer Buddhism. Clifford Geertz asks, "How do men of religious sensibility react when . . . traditions falter?" (1968:3; also
1966). Geertz suggests that people who undergo a progressive increase in doubt question their belief "unconsciously and intermit-
tently"—"its depth, its strength, its hold upon them—not its
validity." The question shifts for individuals from "What shall I
believe?" to "How shall I believe what I believe?" (1968:61).

Certainly for Cambodians this last question is critical and has
implications both for people who remain in their own culture and
for those who fled (for example, how to create valid places and
ways for belief in the United States). But some Cambodians also
ask, "What shall I believe?" Phath's response is to reject the traditional answer of karmic law, at least for now: "If it had been
only myself, I could believe the explanation was my karma, but I
cannot believe this for my whole country." For her, finding adequate answers in traditional religion is problematic: "Buddhism
says, 'when you know suffering, you can find peace.'" She is aware
of the seriousness of questioning traditional answers; however, she
continues, the "Cambodian people have had enough suffering but
they cannot find peace" (Hansen and Phath 1987:11).

Certainly the law of karma does not satisfy Phath: "In my opin-
ion, if people emphasize loving kindness and think less about the
law of karma, there will be a reduction of suffering because people
acting out of loving kindness will create social justice in their

community"(26). Phath thinks that "there are no answers to suffering but only memories, explanations, questions, and maybe the healing result of letting each other talk together." She adds: "Cambodians say, 'only you yourself can help yourself.' This is a Buddhist proverb. But in the case of this experience, people must help each other find an answer in themselves" (11). Phath is still searching.

So is Ngor. On the last page of his autobiography, Ngor finds comfort in the thought that in the future he will be able to reach some peace about the Khmer Rouge period: "Someday when Cambodia is free, I will return to the leaning *sdao* tree on the hillock in the rice fields. With me will be Buddhist monks. . . . We will pray for Huot and her mother and my parents and family, and for all those who lost their lives. Then maybe their souls will be at peace. And maybe mine will be too" (1987:466).

And in the last paragraph of her book, Mam Teeda Butt describes how she will regain her significance, her meaning: "Repeatedly, the Khmer Rouge told us that we were insignificant, that to destroy us was no loss. Revenge in the Western sense can be a destructive force in the life of a wronged person, but for Cambodians revenge has a different meaning. By our actions, by what we can accomplish, we intend to show that we do have significance. When we have proven the Khmer Rouge wrong in their assessment of our culture and of us as individuals, our revenge will be complete" (Criddle and Mam 1987:286).

Mam, like Phath and Ngor, continues to search for answers.

Difficulty of Explanation

The Khmer use a variety of traditional and novel explanations to cope with their holocaust experiences. These answers vary from person to person, often according to individual situations. What is immediately obvious is their dilemma.

As refugees, Khmer in the United States face a new world: the realignment of all that has been, is, should be, and will be. Moreover, the international conflict over resolution of the Cambodian situation, and the continued threat to the country by the Khmer

Rouge, lead Khmer to the conclusion that their past is unique and
that explanation for this past is virtually impossible.

A new factor Khmer refugees must face is an awareness of new
information with which they can work, a new realization that the
world is larger than previously realized and that new comparisons
can be drawn. Khmer refugees must deal with the secularization of
western societies and incompatible world views. Khmer Buddhists
now coexist as a tiny, relatively powerless minority among Christians, those who have lost faith, and those who have never believed. They live surrounded by people whose *kâm* allowed them to
have survived Pol Pot, people who are not Buddhist, most of whom
continued to be unaware that there is such a being as a Khmer
Buddhist, just as Khmer Buddhists previously had no idea that
people in any significant number did not hold assumptions in common with them. Cambodians may have known that such people
existed, but they seldom encountered them, were not surrounded
by them, and were not forced to adapt to their ways to survive.

Khmer in the United States become aware of this new information in vastly differing ways and use an expanding range of reactions and solutions to the problem of legitimizing their faith. This
we see as Khmer search not only within the traditional Khmer
Buddhism that they are able to reestablish in the resettlement
country, but as they search among new religions. The passage of
time does not ease the reexamination of their assumptions about
existence and their religion. Many Khmer in the United States become increasingly concerned with religious issues and ultimate
questions. As their children settle into American ways, Khmer
adults become aware of the limitations and realities for their own
generation of migrants. This realization makes them ask: Why
have these things happened? Why have they happened to *me?*

Another aspect of description/explanation difficulties for
Khmer refugees is their reexamination of previous and newly available terminology. Believers facing new data in a anew environment
can use their traditional vocabularies for new experiences and for
drawing comparisons about old experiences. Conversely, they can
use new terms for new experiences and for drawing comparisons
about familiar ones. These words themselves contribute to the def-

inition of experience—for Khmer refugees, an increasing recognition by themselves and others that their experiences *did* occur and in the ways they describe. For example, Khmer refugees apply the word "holocaust" to the Khmer Rouge experience, noting the ways in which the Khmer situation resembled the holocaust of World War II: the destruction of large numbers of people, the perceived lack of awareness or caring by neighboring peoples, the treatment of victims as completely without worth. Words such as "holocaust" gain importance as they link an individual's experiences to those of others in a historical and cultural context.

Khmer refugees also face unprecedented questions of legitimization in regard to both traditional and novel ways of religious thinking. As Stanley J. Tambiah notes, historical literary "texts and knowledge have a referential and legitimating function" for people, "even if they themselves have no direct access to them" (1970:4). Certainly the wider context of Khmer Buddhism in time and space (its origin, history, expansion) has served in traditional Cambodia as a primary source of legitimization for both literate clergy and uneducated peasant. As has been seen, Khmer Buddhism continues to do so in their new environment. It is, however, becoming increasingly ineffectual as older Khmer forget what they knew of Buddhist texts and have less access to Buddhist lettered men (because there are fewer of them and they are scattered over much larger areas), and as the young are taught less and less of their religious tradition.

A shift in knowledge, terminologies that appear and fade, and legitimacy that often seems to operate capriciously: this is what is involved in believing for Khmer refugees and for others in similar situations. While Khmer stray from the traditional conceptualizations and practices of Khmer Buddhism, they return, again and again, to that which they know best. While it often leaves them dissatisfied, it is what they know, what they can best hold on to.

Finally, the ways Khmer refugees choose to answer their questions continue to vary, whether within a traditional context of Khmer Buddhism, a new context of some form of American Christianity, some folding together of the two, or another way of thinking and explaining. This variation is not just between systems of belief, but within them; thus Khmer Buddhists will disagree with one another on all aspects of Khmer Buddhism in the United States, and their beliefs will themselves vary from day to day.

It is not good enough to say that Khmer have developed alternate explanations for framing their lives during and after Pol Pot, that they have found answers in a variety of conceptual sets to explain the events that have occurred to them. This is true, but not sufficient. It is also important to recognize that Khmer refugees in the United States continue to ask a range of questions that continue to bother them, questions most of them would never have thought to ask until their lives were turned upside down. These questions continue to be addressed, answered, then brought up again.

CHAPTER SEVEN

Khmer Proverbs:
Images and Rules

Karen Fisher-Nguyen

The study of proverbs in a particular culture can illuminate the observance of social rules expressed in concise and often witty statements. Using condensed story lines and familiar images shared by the audience, proverbs seemed to embody traditional wisdom. In his discussion of the universal structure of proverbs, Roger D. Abrahams (1972:122) states that it is this apparent collective wisdom that is most important in making a proverb persuasive. For this reason, proverbs frequently serve as impersonal suggestions for accepted time-proven approaches to common problems and daily frustrations, but are uttered without the risk of personal involvement. What makes this form of apparent traditional wisdom so appealing is not only the forcefulness of the message but the fact that this message is conveyed with an economy of words and the use of poetic devices such as binary composition, rhyme, and metaphor.[1]

In this chapter I take a first step toward the understanding of Khmer social rules and shared images by looking at recurrent themes in a collection of over two hundred Khmer proverbs taken from a variety of written and oral sources.[2] I also look briefly at the contexts in which these themes are relevant.

Khmer literature about proverbs offer several labels for the type of expressions under consideration here. Among them are *pheasĭt* and *sopheasĭt* (words of Indic origin literally meaning "correct speech"), *pĕak chăs* (sayings of elders), *pĕak bauran* (ancient sayings), *pĕak tŭmneay* (traditional sayings), and *Pŭtthăpheasĭt* and *Pŭtth tŭmneay* (sayings and predictions of the Buddha).

Some of the sources of these proverbs are recognized as the morals or themes of familiar stories, many of which can be found in the collection of moralistic fables known as the *Kotĭlôk,* or Art of Good Conduct. Most of these stories can be traced back to works of Indic origin, but some are entirely Khmer in origin.[3] A second source is the important set of didactic poems known collectively as the *Chbăp.* In particular, the "Chbăp Pĕak Chăs," or "Traditional Morality," is often cited as a source of well-known proverbs.[4] Still other proverbs can be found in the collection of Khmer folk tales and legends known as the *Brâchŭm Reuang Préng Khmae,* some of which are attributed to Indic sources as well as to stories told by wise elders and ancestors which were written down and kept in village temples throughout Cambodia.[5] Another source is Buddhist works, in particular, the sayings and predictions of the Buddha.[6]

Several informants distinguish the labels of these sources according to what they consider to be the source of a particular saying (e.g., sayings attributed to the Buddha). Others, however, say that there is no difference and that all the labels are just different ways of saying the same thing. What appears to be important about the different labels, regardless of the one used, is that each implies a sanctioned respected source, whether it be a work of Indic origin, a moralistic story passed down from elders and ancestors, or the teachings of the Buddha.

In prerevolutionary Cambodia, proverbs were held in such high regard that they played a role in the public education of children. Not only could they be found scattered throughout many of the required teaching materials, such as primers, novels, and the *Chbăp,* but the study of proverbs in and of themselves was also part of the school curriculum at certain levels.[7] In refugee camps in Thailand and the Philippines, proverbs also appeared prominently in campwide Khmer publications and could be found painted on the walls of public facilities to serve as an inspiration to the youth.[8]

Among the dominant themes found in the proverbs, and the ones to be discussed here, are: (1) praise and encouragement of admired qualities; (2) admonition about undesirable qualities and the problems they can lead to; (3) respect for tradition and the tendency toward conservatism; (4) comments on status and interpersonal relationships; (5) the family, with particular emphasis on women; (6) Buddhist notions of moderation and Karma; and (7) the power of speech and language.

1. Several qualities are admired and encouraged in the proverbs. The first is humility, expressed in the following proverb:

> *Ngoey skât aon dǎk krŏap.*

> The immature rice stalk stands erect, while
> the mature stalk, heavy with grain, bends over.

Khmer parents teach their children to humble themselves and show respect toward superiors and elders by stooping over whenever they walk near them. In Khmer, the word *aon* is used to describe this show of respect as well as to describe the bending over of the mature rice stalk. Seen in the rice plant, it is an indication of the bounty, richness, and maturity of the grain in a person; it indicates a good upbringing, good character, and respect.

The next admirable quality is discretion, seen in a proverb from a well-known folk tale about an unfaithful wife who is found out:

> *Aus touk mǐn aoey l'an chǎp trey ban mǐn aoey l'ǎk tĕuk.*

> Drag a boat without leaving a trace;
> catch a fish without muddying the water.[9]

The point here is to avoid calling unwanted attention to anything you do. If you do something that is obvious for all to see, however, you should face up to it and not be so foolish as to try to hide it:

> *Dǎmrey slǎp kŏm yok chang'e mok bǎng.*

> Don't try to hide a dead elephant
> with a winnowing basket.

Adaptability and flexibility are also desirable qualities, especially in new situations and around new people. By adapting to

your new surroundings you will avoid calling unwanted attention
to yourself. These qualities are emphasized in this proverb:

> *Chaul stĕung tam bât chaul srŏk tam brâtés.*
>
> Negotiate a river by following its bends;
> enter a country by following its customs.

2. Admonitions about undesirable and potentially problematic
qualities abound in the proverbs. The first is pride, which can lead
to ambitiousness. Both are discouraged in numerous proverbs,
such as:

> *Kŏm yok mékh trŏap ângkŭy.*
>
> Don't take the sky to make a
> seat for yourself.

> *Khluon teap kŏm taong dai khley kŏm chhông aop brâva phnŭm.*
>
> Small one, don't stand up so tall;
> and you with the short arms,
> don't try to embrace the mountain.

Pride leads to behavior inappropriate to one's status, something to
be avoided always:

> *Dămrey chŭh thŭm kŏm chŭh tam dămrey.*
>
> The elephant has a huge shit;
> don't try to shit like the elephant.

> *Touk touc kŏm brâdauch nĭng touk thvae.*
>
> A small boat shouldn't
> try to be like a large boat.

> *Kŏm phtŭk tam thvae.*
>
> Don't take rich people as examples.

Khmers are advised not to be timid because timidity hinders achievement:

Khmah krou kmean brachnha khmah brâpŭan kmean kaun.

If you're timid with your teacher, you won't learn;
if you're timid with your wife, you won't have children.

Stupidity is also to be avoided, but being knowledgeable can have its problems, too, especially if it leads to loudness and boasting. In both instances, advice is offered in the following two versions of a single proverb:

Mngai nĕung cheh aoey ké kaot mngai nĕung chhaot aoey ké anĕt.

If you know a lot, know enough to make them respect you;
if you are stupid, be stupid enough to make them pity you.

Baoe kach kach aoey ké kaot baoe chhaot chhaot aoey ké anĕt.

If you're mean, be mean enough so that they respect you;
if you are stupid, be stupid enough so that they pity you.

Stupidity and foolishness can also lead to unnecessary complications and further problems later on. In one proverb, from a folk tale about a foolish wife, there is a warning against such unnecessary complications and encouragement to look for simple solutions to problems:

Ântŭang vêng kŏm băch rok chnăng vêng.

If you have a long eel,
don't look for a long pot in which to cook it.[10]

Khmers are also advised to be careful not to believe in others too quickly. Several proverbs advise against being naive and too trusting without careful consideration.

Kŏm aoey cheua mékh kŏm aoey cheua phkay
kŏm aoey cheua kaun tha kmean sâhay
kŏm aoey cheua mtay tha kmean bămnŏl.

Don't believe the sky; don't believe the stars;
don't believe your daughter when she says she has no lover;
don't believe your mother when she says she has no debts.

Also, they are advised against trusting people least worthy of trust:

> Monŭh khŏeng kŏm aoey leang chan
> monŭs khlean kŏm aoey dăm bay.

> Don't trust an angry man to wash dishes,
> or rice to a hungry man.

> Kŏm yok pong mŏan tôv phnhoe nĕung k'aek.

> Don't send an egg with a crow.

Men are advised to be careful about women:

> Chămney chngănh kŏm tŭk s'aek
> brâpŭan chămlaek kŏm aoey daoe kraoy.

> Just as you shouldn't try to set aside delicious food for tomorrow,
> if your wife is desirable don't have her walk behind you.

Those in positions of authority are warned not to trust those under
them completely, as expressed in this proverb:

> Chma mĭn nôv kântŏ laoeng reach.

> When the cat is not around,
> the mouse ascends the throne.

Finally, Khmers should consider carefully words that sound too
sweet. Women are advised not to believe the sweet talk of a man:

> Tĕuk hau mĭn dael hăt sbâth brŏh kŏm aoey cheua.

> Just as the water never ceases to flow,
> so you should not believe the promises of a man.[11]

In another, sweet words mask an evil heart:

> *Chĕt chea tévotot mŏat chea tévota.*

> An evil heart, but an angel's mouth.

Both admired and discouraged qualities often appear together in a single proverb, as an emphasis on the contrast between the two. In the following, patience and perseverance are praised and have a desired result, while impatience and haste result in misfortune:

> *Tăk tăk pénh bămpŭang chhŏng chhŏng kămpŭap ăs.*

> Drop by drop the vessel fills;
> pouring causes it all to spill.

3. Another theme is the importance of tradition, including respect for the ways things have always been done. Trying something new is not encouraged:

> *Phlauv viech kŏm baoh bằng phlauv trẳng kŏm daoe haong
> daoe daoy konlong tâmray nĕak chăs bauran.*

> Don't reject the crooked road and don't take the straight one;
> instead, take the road traveled by the ancestors.

Those who choose to ignore tradition, thinking they know more than those who came before, are warned that they may not be happy with the consequences, as in this proverb from a folk tale in which a man and woman try to outsmart a fortuneteller:

> *Kŏm ang uot atma tmăh tâmra brach préng neay.*

> Don't brag about yourself;
> you may be ashamed by traditional wisdom.[12]

4. Khmers view themselves as links in a chain, interconnected with those around them. In fact, in a reference to oneself or to an

addressee in conversation, the referring term used, be it a pronoun, title, or kinship term, makes a statement about the relationship. A large number of referring expressions are possible in Khmer, and social implications reside in each. Proper observance of such relationships is crucial in Khmer society, not only in the way one speaks but also in the way one behaves. This importance is reflected in the many proverbs that refer to interpersonal relationships and how the individual fits into the scheme of things.

Khmers are advised not to prejudge others, because a person's status may someday change, as given in the following proverb:

> *Trŏk trŏk nĕak srŏk moel ngeay*
> *rolŏas kouth khchay mean ŭd mean phŏan.*

> The stupid person, scorned by neighbors,
> may suddenly become wealthy and wise.[13]

The timid should not be prejudged as weak because they too are powerful in their own way:

> *Mŏeh mŏeh keh chnăng bay thlŭh.*

> The timid person can pierce the rice pot.

In another proverb Khmers are warned that there is danger in prejudging those one should be wary of:

> *Khla krap kŏm tha khla sămpĕah.*

> If the tiger lies down quietly before you,
> don't say it respects you.

Khmers are also advised not to point out another's faults, especially if they too are guilty of such faults:

> *Leang kouth aeng mĭn chrĕah phâng tôv leang kouth ké.*

> You haven't yet wiped your own ass clean,
> yet you go to wipe someone else's.

Several proverbs deal with the relationship between superiors/ strong and inferiors/weak. First, the strong and fortunate are encouraged to be responsible for taking care of those less fortunate, as expressed in these two proverbs:[14]

> *Něak mean rěaksa khsăt dauch sămpŭat pŏat pi krav.*
>
> The rich should take care of the poor
> like the cloth which surrounds you.
>
> *Něak brach rěaksa khlav dauch sămpôv nouv sămpan.*
>
> The wise should watch over the ignorant
> like the ships do a sampan.

In doing so, the wise will not only accumulate merit, a topic I return to later, but they will also have many waiting to serve them, as expressed in the following:

> *Těuk trâchěak trey phtŏm.*
>
> If the water is cold the fish will flourish.

Proper behavior in dealing with superiors is always necessary, which includes observing the chain-of-command, not trying to get around it, as advised in the following:

> *Kŏm baoh santouch rŭmlong phnŭm.*
>
> Don't throw the fishing line across the mountain.

Going up against one's superiors is considered futile because losing is inevitable:

> *Pong mŏan kŏm chŭal něung thmâ.*
>
> Don't hit a stone with an egg.

Often when a superior falters, those below succeed:

Khlôk lĭch ămbaeng ântaet.

When the hollow gourd sinks, the clay pot floats.[15]

5. Many proverbs deal with the family, with particular emphasis on women. The importance of the wife and mother to her family is seen in numerous proverbs. The virtuous and exemplary woman (*srey krŭap lĕakkh*) seen in folk tales also appears in the proverbs. She determines the happiness and prosperity of her family, as expressed in the following:

> *Trŏap kŭang tbĕt srey cheh sămchai tŭk*
> *phtĕah thŭm srânŏk tbĕt lĕakkh srey chea.*

> Wealth is there because the woman knows
> how to save and be frugal; a house is comfortable
> and happy because the wife has a good character.[16]

Husbands are advised to listen to their wives because of their frugal nature, and those that do not have to suffer the consequences:

> *Mĭn cheua pĕak srey ăs srauv pouch.*

> If you do not listen to the advice of a woman,
> you'll not have any rice seed next year.

She is also expected to support and help her husband:

> *Sămnap yông dey srey yông brŏs.*

> The rice seedling draws the dirt to it in clumps;
> the woman supports the man.

For the child, she is more important than the father:

> *Sauv slăp ba kŏm aoey slăp mé*
> *sauv lŭang tĕuk kântal tonlé*
> *kŏm aoey phloeng chheh phtĕah.*

Better to lose one's father, than one's mother;
it's better to lose one's goods when the boat sinks in the
       middle of the river,
than lose one's goods when the house burns down.

6. The influence of Buddhism is seen in the proverbs. Moderation is encouraged in all aspects of life. In particular, Khmers are encouraged not to act in haste, but to take things slowly and calmly:

Khlean kŏm al si.

If you're hungry, don't be in a hurry to eat.

Baoe leu phko kŏm al chăk tĕuk bămpŭang chaol.

If you hear the thunder, don't be in a hurry
to throw out the rain water you have stored.

Khoenh chhoe pŭk kŏm al tomlĕak trâpôk ângkŭy.

When you see a rotten tree,
don't be in a hurry to sit on it.

Ké khŏh kŏm al â ké sato kŏm al uot.

If they make a mistake, don't rejoice;
if they show you respect,
don't be in a hurry to brag about it.

This caution does not mean that Khmers are discouraged from taking action. On the contrary, if the time is right, one should act:

Thvoe srae tŏan ktav dey chăng srey tŏan ktav chĕt.

Grow rice when the ground is warm;
pursue a woman when you feel the passion.

Although moderation is encouraged, excess of any kind is held to be the source of many problems. One proverb affords two interpretations along these lines, depending on the reading of the word *l'â*. In the first rendering it means "beautiful," in the second, "good":

> *Kô leuan sŏek kâ srey l'â sŏek kouth.*

> A strong cow (that is used too much)
> soon wears out its neck;
> a beautiful woman is soon worn out (by men).

> A strong cow (that is used too much)
> soon wears out its neck;
> a good, virtuous woman works too hard
> and soon gets worn out.

Karma is also important in the determination of one's status and destiny:

> *Thvoe bŏn ban bŏn thvoe bap ban bap.*

> If you sow good, you'll get good;
> if you sow bad, you'll get bad.

Another proverb points out that the creatures of the earth are all artisans of their own destiny:

> *Krâpoe slăp nĕung sbaek kămphlanh slăp nĕung mŏat*
> *khvaek slăp nĕung ach.*

> The crocodile dies because of skin (and its value);
> the *kămphlanh* fish dies because of its call
> (which reveals its location to the fisherman);
> the crabeater bird dies because of its dung
> (which accumulates beneath its tree and
> reveals its location at night to the hunter).

7. The power of language reflected in the proverbs is the last theme I consider. Language used wisely can be powerful and effective, but used imprudently it can lead to trouble and shame:

Ŏem cheang iem sngiem cheang sămdey.

Better to close your mouth than open it;
better to be quiet than to speak.

Roneap băk krŏan chuoh tae mŏat vea huoh vea băng brăk.

If the lattice breaks, it is easy to repair;
but if you talk too much, it will cost you dearly.

Chŭmpŭap choeng kăng băt baoe kămpŭap mŏat băng brăk.

If you misstep, you can retrace your steps,
but if you are careless with your words,
it will cost you dearly.

Ântat chea atĭ kânlâng băng trŏap thŭan phâng piprŭah ântat.

The power of the tongue is unlimited;
if you lose all it is also because of your tongue.

Being able to speak correctly in all situations is highly valued
and is often compared to other items of value, as in these two
proverbs:

Monŭh yok sămdey dămrey yok phlŭk.

Man has speech; the elephant has its tusks.

Sauv băng brăk muoy thăng kŏm aoey băng pĕak.

It's better to lose money than to waste words.

The themes expressed in these proverbs are presented in everyday language. There is little use of *pĕak vobbâthŏa* (literary words)
that are so often used in writing, yet not always understood by all
readers. The images used in the proverbs to make them immediately understood are familiar ones that Khmers come into contact
with on a regular, if not daily basis, including all aspects of rice
production, animals of all kinds, both savage and domestic,

common modes of transportation, plants and trees, rivers and fish, natural occurrences (e.g., rain, clouds), familiar landscape, and household items.[17] The simplicity of the language and the familiarity of the illustrative image enhance the persuasiveness of the proverb; and it is by studying the message itself, including its theme, that we begin to understand its importance.

CHAPTER EIGHT

Metaphors of the
Khmer Rouge

John Marston

In *The Stones Cry Out*, Molyda Szymusiak recounts an incident near the end of the Democratic Kampuchea period when she observed people being tortured by soldiers (*yôthea*) in an orange grove close to the place she was sleeping: "I couldn't resist the desire to see what was going on. It was a changing of the guard: three *yôthea* came to laugh in the faces of the tortured men. 'So you don't feel too well? You'll make it. Just wait, you'll feel better in a little while.' These sugary words, that irony—I recognized all that, it was the way the *yôthea* talked" (1986:182). This is an extreme example and a very gruesome one—perhaps it removes us far away from the question of how the Khmer Rouge used language in less extreme situations. But it does illustrate the idea that there was something about the way that the Khmer Rouge used language which had consistency: it was a recognizable style.

Two stylistic issues will be addressed here. First, I make an attempt to classify what refugees have considered to be language typical of the Pol Pot period. I intuitively feel, however, that it is not enough to dismiss the Khmer Rouge as evil. We must try to come to grips with the specific *tone* of that evil, as it is manifested in the language. Through such analysis, we may find hints of the underlying system of thought.

There are many kinds of metaphors and many frameworks for looking at them. One basic way of viewing metaphor is in terms of the possibility it creates for taking what is already familiar—from the domain of the past—to refer to something new. To the extent that this happens, there will be implicit in the metaphor a link between the past and the present. Antonio Gramsci writes, "Usually when one new conception of the world succeeds another, the earlier language continues to be used but is used metaphorically. All language is a continuous process of metaphors, and the history of semantics is an aspect of the history of culture: language is at the same time a living thing and a museum of the fossils of life and civilisation" (1957:110–11). In other words, metaphor is implicit in any innovation of vocabulary.

A revolution is by definition a break in the continuity of culture and is conceived as such to the extent that the people involved perceive the existence of a break. This definition does not imply, of course, that the society as it exists during and after a revolution does not continue to have culture, or that the culture does not have links to the past. Even with the enormous discontinuities of the Khmer Rouge revolution, there were such links, and these can be illustrated in a broad way by linguistic phenomena. Language does change in the course of a revolution, either by a process of evolution or by conscious reform, but it remains in some sense the same language. One reason for examining the metaphors of the Khmer Rouge is that understanding the process of metaphors may be a way to grasp the progression of one conception of the world to another.

Another useful framework for considering metaphor is proposed by George Lakoff and Mark Johnson in *Metaphors We Live By* (1980). They are concerned with the question of how the repertoire of metaphors in a language are patterned around underlying metaphorical assumptions that shape the way we are able to think about things. They distinguish between conventional metaphors and new metaphors, and are concerned primarily with the former. They do point out that innovations in metaphor can represent a deliberate attempt to shape the way the world is perceived: "New metaphors, like conventional metaphors, can have the power to define reality. They do this through a coherent network of entailments that highlight some features of reality and hide others. The acceptance of the metaphor, which forces us to focus only on those aspects of our experience that it highlights, leads us to view the entailments of the metaphor as being true" (157).

Another idea relevant to our discussion is that metaphor, particularly insofar as it is a new metaphor, tends to lend dignity to the thing it refers to, implicitly acknowledging a connection to a cosmic pattern of things. The exceptions to this relationship, when metaphor is used humorously or derogatorily, are playing off the basic assumption that a metaphor dignifies.

I begin with a single metaphor that is dramatic and speaks in general terms about the nature of the Khmer Rouge regime:

Ângka mean phnêk mnŏah (Ith Sarin 1977).

Ângka has the eyes of a pineapple.

Briefly stated, it means that the revolutionary organization, ângka, knows everything that is going on—it can see in all directions, just as the eyes of the pineapple point in all directions.

The word ângka has a complicated set of implications in and of itself. It means literally "organization" and is often used to mean nothing more than this. The root of the word, âng, comes from a Sanskrit word that means "limb of the body" or "constituent part" (Headley 1977). The same root is found in two other words associated with the Democratic Kampuchea period: ângkopheap—a word used to designate broad social groupings—and âng brâchŭm—a word used to refer to small-scale meetings.

Although ângka was not a new word in the revolutionary period, refugees sometimes report having felt some confusion during the first weeks of the regime about what it signified—perhaps either because it was drawn from a more elevated register of vocabulary than they were used to or because the way it was now being used was peculiarly different. Szymusiak (1986), for instance, writes that at first she thought the word referred to a person. During Democratic Kampuchea as, in fact, among Cambodians in the United States now, the word ângka was often used in a way that personified it.

May Someth writes with great irony: "To celebrate the completion of the dam, the performing group came to entertain us. They sang of our love for the *Angkar*—it was as wide as the sea, it had no boundary. We were masters of our work. There was no more exploitation. We could do whatever we wanted. The canals were the veins of the *Angkar.* We were no longer reliant on rain. We could produce as much rice as we wanted" (1986:177).

The following quotation, from a speech reprinted in a Khmer Rouge newspaper, does not specifically use the word *ângka* but, similarly, uses the metaphor of the collectivity representing a body:

> *Dauchneh yoeng trauv pongrĕung smarâtey sângkom nĭyom tiet oay tôv chea sâsai nhĕak sâmauhâpheap.*

> Therefore we must make more solid the socialist consciousness so that it becomes the trembling nerves and veins of the collectivity (*Tŭang Bâdĕvât* 1976:29).

I pointed out that there was an ambiguity of reference in the use of the word *ângka.* Since no one really knew who or what *ângka* was, it could not be held responsible for its actions. It was commonly represented to people at the bottom of the social hierarchy as a vague entity above them. At other times people were told that they themselves, the population, were *ângka.* In a footnote to the forced confessions of Hu Nim, Ben Kiernan (1988:340–41) notes that in one place the word *ângka* seems to refer to Pol Pot himself.

In the statement, "*Ângka* has the eyes of a pineapple," Gramsci's principle is illustrated even in the fact that a pineapple, something familiar, is taken to define metaphorically a new social entity. But a more culturally resonant way in which the idea could be said to be applied is found in the similarity of the image of the pineapple looking out in all directions to the image, associated with the Bayon at Angkor Thom, of a single head with four faces looking out in all directions. I propose that, consciously or not, the Khmer Rouge metaphor of the pineapple recalls this icon. Certainly visitors climbing up to Angkor Thom are impressed by the same feeling evoked by the expression about the pineapple, of a presence peering at them constantly from all directions.

The idea that a symbol associated with the Angkor empire would be invoked during Democratic Kampuchea is consistent with the fact that, during that period, pictures of Angkor Wat were displayed in public places, and songs drew parallels between the glories of the new regime and those of Angkor. A section on tour-

ism in a Democratic Kampuchea "Four-Year Plan to Build Socialism in All Fields"—which speaks in the same breath of tourists
visiting Angkor Wat, Angkor Thom, and Banteay Srey, and their
visiting "the system of dikes, irrigation channels, canals, ricefields,
vegetable gardens, fishing areas" (Chandler, Kiernan, and Boua
1988:105)—suggests that the Democratic Kampuchea program to
build up the irrigation system was related to a conception that irrigation was the basis of the glories of Angkor.

The way that representations of the head with four faces is used
among Cambodians in the United States as a symbol of the homeland is evidence of its complex connotations for the Khmer. Whatever the purposes of the original creators of the Bayon, the image
is now sometimes used to invoke Buddhist principles and to expli-
cate ideas about the proper nature of authority, including the relation of the parent to the child.[1] The figure with four faces is
reproduced on the cover of a United Nations High Commissioner
for Refugees (UNHCR) textbook used in refugee camps and seems
to suggest the personage of a parent or a teacher.

One Khmer man, speaking in English, said that the meaning of
the statement "*Ângka* has the eyes of a pineapple" is that the spirit
of *ângka* was everywhere. The metaphor is reported as having
been used during the Democratic Kampuchea period in public
meetings: people were admonished that they should not break
rules or resist authorities, because "*Ângka* has the eyes of a pineapple" and would know whatever they did. Used in this way, the
metaphor describes not just *ângka* but contributes toward creating
ângka as a conceptual entity. It is difficult to grasp exactly what
tone it would have conveyed or to divorce it from our own cultural
icons of "Big Brother is watching" or the Panopticon as described
by Michel Foucault (1979:195–228). I was surprised when one
man interviewed—who happened to have had close ties to the
Khmer Rouge—laughed when he repeated the phrase. It is a
homely conceit, even though it is clear that it was intended to inspire fear and that it did so. The incongruity, perhaps containing
an element of irony, comes in the use of a pineapple to inspire fear.
This incongruity is typical, I think, of one aspect of the way the
Khmer Rouge used language, the same type of phenomenon Soth
Polin was talking about when he wrote that for the Khmer Rouge

"gentleness entwines with cruelty to the point where they become confused" (1980:43). Something modest, everyday, and homely is taken and used in a way that somehow suggests something fearful, overwhelming, and awesome.

Lakoff and Johnson's book on metaphor is to a great extent concerned with finding ways in which clusters of conventional metaphors can be shown to be related by underlying metaphorical concepts. Much of what was regarded as characteristic in the language of the Khmer Rouge can be organized into patterns of this sort.

I have elsewhere discussed (Marston with Duong 1988) a pattern in the use of metaphors which projected the image of the family onto other social units: the work group, the cooperative, or *ângka*, in such a way that these units were attributed the authority that was once assigned to the parent. One of the many examples of this is a Democratic Kampuchea song written down for me by a refugee.

> *Ôv Ôv ângka dael mean kŭn kŭn nĕak saen thngŭan brâman*
> *cămpŭah brâcheachŭan cămpŭah roup kaun daoy*
> > *laek daoy laek.*
> *Nĕak ban pyeayeam ăp rŭm kaun hăk dauch chea kbaun*
> > *khăm pyeayeam chlâng tĕuk*
> *sa chŏh sa laoeng hăt neuay mtech mta svăh svaeng lŭh tra*
> > *kaun ban chôk chay.*

> Oh, Oh, *ângka* that has loving kindness, the loving kindness
> > of someone great without measure
> for the race and the people, and especially for the children—
> someone who has persevered to train the children, just like
> > a raft trying to cross the water,
> back and forth, so exhausted, it strives until the children
> > have victory.

The following lines, from the song "Children of the New Kampuchea" in a Democratic Kampuchea songbook, suggest the same thing more subtly.

> *Yoeng khnhŏm kŏma mean sŏphĕak mongkŭal*
> *dâ sŏkhâdŏm dael rŭas nôv thlai thla*

kraom ka krŭap krong kăk ktav dâ mohĭmea
robăs bâdĕvât Kâmpŭchea dâ phleu svang.

We the children have the good fortune
to live the rest of our time in precious harmony
under the affectionate care
of the Kampuchean revolution, immense, most clear
and shining.
(*Chămrieng Bâdĕvât*, vol. 3, n.d.:33–34)

François Pouchaud (1978) and others have noted that in Democratic Kampuchea military terminology was widely used to refer to the social activities of peacetime, such as campaigns to grow rice or to dig irrigation canals. In dividing the work of the population, authorities spoke of the front lines (*sâmârâphoum mŭkh*), which did more arduous work, and the rear lines (*sâmârâphoum kraoy*). The basic work unit was a *kâng*, a military grouping, and the most arduous work was performed by mobile teams, *kâng câlat*, also a military term. The rhetoric of the Khmer Rouge is full of references to launching offensives (*veay sâmrŏk*), to struggling in a military sense (*brâyut*), to fighting onward (*tâsou*), and to persevering (*btechnha*).[2]

The song "Children of the New Kampuchea," quoted from earlier, uses military terminology to describe study: (*brâyŭt pongrik nouv ka yŭal dŏeng*), "struggling to increase understanding and knowledge." Speaking of children's study, farm labor, and work in the village, it says:

Yoeng khnhŏm kŏma bâdĕvât Kâmpŭchea
tăng chĕt btechnha khpŭas khpŭang bămphŏt
khĕt khăm pongrik sâmâtthâpheap brâyŭt
nĭng chŭmho bâdĕvât aoy l'â ât khchaoh.

We the children of the revolution
make the supreme resolution to strive
to increase our ability to battle,
and make the stand of the revolution perfect.
(*Chămrieng Bâdĕvât*, vol. 3, n.d.:33–34)

A Khmer woman, in her unpublished memoirs of the period, writes about being moved from one work area to another:

Khnhŏm prom tĕang b'aun srey nĭng kmeng kmeng cheang khnhŏm chǎmnuon buon nĕak tiet ban trauv "ângka chǎt tǎng laoeng" daoembey tôv "brâyŭt knŏng câlâna ktav" nôv di nôh.

I and my younger sister and four other girls younger than I were "designated by *Angkar*" to go up in order to "combat in the hot movement" there (Siv 1987:pt. 5, 11).

I think there was a touch of the Democratic Kampuchea military style, maybe used ironically, in the way one of my informants told how he and his wife remained married even though others, whose marriages had also been forcibly arranged by the state shortly before 1979, had separated. "It was just me, together with my wife, who kept fighting the good fight (*tâsou*)."

It could be argued that military forms of social organization were applied to the general population. The underlying metaphor seems to have been that the society was like an army at war. The metaphor also functioned to remind the "new people" of the distinction between them and the people who had actually fought in the revolution. The revolutionary struggle was constantly held up as a standard the population had to live up to.

There are also consistent patterns in the use of metaphors during the Democratic Kampuchea period which deal with building and standing. Perhaps these can be seen as an extension of the military metaphor. While these are really two different kinds of metaphors—those of building and those of standing—they occur in similar contexts, and both evoke the image of something rising above a base. One common Democratic Kampuchean usage combines the two metaphors and speaks of "building a standpoint" (*kâsang kôl chŭmho*), which could perhaps be paraphrased as consolidating one's position.

These metaphors operate on two levels: the society and the individual. It is perhaps not surprising that the Democratic Kampuchea regime spoke of building (*kâsang*) the country. The people, usually peasants, who were in liberated zones before the overthrow of Phnom Penh and sometimes called "old people," were also called "base citizens" (*brâcheachŭan moulâdthan*)—"base" in the sense of a base on which something is built or a base of operations. A Democratic Kampuchea newspaper stressed the impor-

tance of agriculture by describing it as something "we stand on."
"We stand on agriculture in order to increase the other areas: industry, factories, iron, oil, etc." (*Yoeng chho loe kâsĕkâm daoembey pângrik phnaek dâtai tiet douch chea oussahâkâm rông câk
daek breng lak; Tuâng bâdĕvât* 1976:53). A Democratic Kampuchea geography text says, "Rice is the base crop and capital for
building and defending the country" (*Srouv chea dămnăm moulâdthan nĭng chea tŭn sămrăp kâsang nĭng kapea brâtés yoeng,*
Cambodia, Ministry of Education 1976:35). Although each of
these is a slightly different metaphor, they show consistency in describing agriculture and the people associated with it as a base. It
is clear from "The Party's Four-Year Plan to Build Socialism in All
Fields" (Chandler, Kiernan, and Boua 1988) that making agriculture the "base" was not just a metaphor, it was economic policy.

The role of youth was considered crucial in Democratic Kampuchea, and, among other ways of describing youth, we occasionally find metaphors that picture their role in building on the base.
A 1973 document translated by Timothy M. Carney says that "the
party has educated, watched, nourished, and *re-educated* youth as
the central force in the revolutionary movement of each era and as
the central force for future national *construction*" (emphasis mine;
Carney 1977:33). One informant said that Democratic Kampuchea authorities referred to children as the "central supporting column of the country" (*sâsâ troung*). This is perhaps in contrast to a
Khmer Buddhist concept that uses another word for column, *prĕah
kânlaong,* to refer to the concept that a person's parents should be
regarded as resembling a deity.

The word *kâsang,* "to build," was also used to describe the
building up of the collectivity, sometimes in expressions that demonstrate an opposition between *kâsang* and words meaning
"to destroy."

Kămchăt kâmmâsĕt eakâchŭan kâsang kâmmâsĕt sâmauhâpheap.

Disburse private property; build up collective property.

Or, to use a conventionalized metaphor that includes the meaning
of the slogan just quoted:

Kămtéc suon tuo kâsang suon ruom.

Destroy the garden of the individual; build a united garden.

The word *kâsang* could also be used with regard to specific classes of people, as in this passage from "The Party's Four-Year Plan to Build Socialism in All Fields":

> Build up concretely, according to background:
> —build workers
> —build peasants
> —build various class layers who are taking up lives as new peasants or workers: intellectuals, petty bourgeois, capitalists, feudal landlords, former government officials. (Chandler, Kiernan, and Boua 1988)

Perhaps the most interesting aspect of these metaphors of building and standing are the parallels between their use in reference to the larger body of society and their use in reference to individual persons. People were told to build themselves (*kâsang khluon*). They were also told to build a standpoint (*kâsang kôl chŭmho*) or to make their stand firm (*pangrĕung kôl chŭmho*). They were told not to have a shaky stand in the manner of imperialists (*kôl chŭmho kŏm trét trôt tam câkrâpot nĭyom*), but to have a self-reliant stand (*kôl chŭmho eakâreach mchăhka*). We recall the lines quoted from the song above: "to strive to increase our ability to battle, and make the stand of the revolution perfect." The repeated references to the importance of a revolutionary stand in Democratic Kampuchean literature gives a striking sense of how important resolve was for the Khmer Rouge. According to one informant, during Democratic Kampuchea people were told that the three things that together constituted *kôl chŭmho* were "discipline, political line, and spirit" (*vĭnay, meakea, sâtĕ'arâm*).

Another expression, apparently quite similar in meaning to the idea of *kâsang kôl chŭmho*, was the idea that *ângka* could "clothe a standpoint" (*bămpĕak kôl chŭmho*) or "clothe and feed a standpoint" (*bămpĕak bămpân kôl chŭmho*). The song "Children of the New Kampuchea" includes the lines "*Yoeng khnhŏm pyeayeam rien saut noyôbay bănpĕak rŏal thngai kôl chŭmho bâdĕvât"* ("We persevere in studying politics / clothing every day our revolutionary stand").

The Cambodian refugees with whom I have talked have been puzzled by this usage themselves, and I do not think that I have yet found an adequate explanation for it. The usage of the expression they generally describe seems to refer to what was supposed to have taken place at political meetings. One informant also mentioned that in the Democratic Kampuchean period the ceremony of marriage involved "clothing a standpoint." Carney (1977:67) translates *bămpĕak bămpân* as "nurture," perhaps suggesting, again, the image of *ângka* as a parental figure clothing and feeding a young child.

But the most commonly reported usage of the word *kâsang*, "to build," is its use as a word that means to criticize formally. I found among Cambodian refugees frequent use of expressions such as "Did they ever *kâsang* you [in the Pol Pot period]?" The English word "reconstruct" can contain some of the political implications of this expression, as in the statement "He was reconstructed," but the specific Democratic Kampuchea usage is slightly different. It refers to a point during a public meeting when a person's fault is pointed out. This occasion may or may not result in punishment. Some refugees say that to have been *kâsang*'d three times meant death. In contrast with the expression *kâsang khluon*, it was clear that, in this instance, someone else was "building" the person rather than the person building himself. This example illustrates the degree to which a word with positive connotations can be used in such a way that it becomes frightening.

A final metaphor related to building is the word *lŭat dăm*, which refers to the process whereby a blacksmith heats iron in a fire to strengthen it and make it usable. This was originally used by Khmer Rouge resistance soldiers to describe the process of hardening themselves in battle. According to one informant, *lŭat dăm* was originally something a person did to himself. Only later did the word come to refer to something applied by external force. For most refugees interviewed, the word *lŭat dăm* referred to the process whereby someone was given more difficult duties as a means of purification. Sometimes it was regarded as a euphemism for "to kill." Like *kâsang*, it sometimes came to mean the opposite of what the words literally signified.

To speak of the metaphors of the Khmer Rouge is a convention that assumes, for the purpose of simplicity, that the Khmer Rouge were a single entity capable of speaking with a single voice, when what was actually involved was a complex range of different people, at different social levels, who used metaphor in a variety of different social situations. Nevertheless, we can say that certain metaphors occur with noticeable frequency in the surviving written materials of the Democratic Kampuchea period, and their saliency is emphasized by the fact that Cambodians also sometimes point to them as typical of the language of the period. Of the metaphors we are considering—metaphors of building and standing, metaphors of war, even the use of a specific image to represent metaphorically a group or a society—none is exclusive to Cambodia or to the language of the Khmer Rouge. Their interest comes not just from the simple fact that they were used, but from the fact that their use at a certain time was regarded as innovative, and the innovation was seen as characteristic of style associated with the Khmer Rouge.

I think that there are at least four directions we can take in considering the significance of metaphors of this kind. One would be to compare the use of these metaphors with the use of similar metaphors in other cultural and historical contexts. Thus, rather than simply characterize the Khmer Rouge usage of military metaphors as representative of a military frame of mind, it would be interesting to investigate whether there is any commonality with other specific contexts in which military metaphors are used, such as, for example, Protestant hymns. Or, it would be interesting to investigate whether there are certain historical contexts that are more likely than others to produce a need to characterize a large, complex society in terms of a single image, such as an all-seeing pineapple. Such discussion is beyond the scope of this paper.

A second direction would be to examine how, within the context of the Democratic Kampuchea period itself, the use of the same metaphor to refer to different things provides a clue to links in a conceptual system. The predominance of metaphors of building and standing is interesting for what it evokes about the Khmer

Rouge emphasis on resolve. But even more suggestive to me is the fact that the same metaphors that are used to talk about the country as a whole are also applied to individual people in the society. Thus, we can ask how the conception of "building" the nation as a whole was related to the conception of individual leaders that they were "building" themselves, and how the "building" of individual leaders and of the entire country was related to the need to "build" the individuals who were part of the general population. This range of significance parallels the range of different meanings of the word *ângka*, which could refer to leadership (the party, or perhaps Pol Pot himself, or an unclearly defined authority) at the same time that it could refer to the entire society or the sum total of its individual members, including the person being addressed. The eyes of the pineapple were simultaneously the eyes of leadership and the eyes of the general population and, perhaps, the eyes of the individual's conscience. Do these conceptual links tell us anything about how power functioned during the period?

A third way of looking at metaphor during the Cambodian revolution is an indicator of links to the past, along the lines of the quotation from Gramsci. We use the past metaphorically to refer to the innovations of the present; perhaps the metaphor then provides an indication of *how* our present concepts are grounded in those of the past. The Khmer Rouge evoked the era of the Angkor empire in their imagery. In subtle ways, they drew on conceptions of traditional Khmer relations within the family and, perhaps, aspects of Buddhism. They certainly drew on the experience of war in the immediate past. The function of the metaphor is, of course, that of a mechanism to transform the past into something serviceable in the present, not just repeat it. The metaphorical link to the past could even entail a reversal—the use of the past to show what is *not* wanted, as in the slogan "Destroy the garden of the individual; build a united garden."

The fourth way in which I believe it is fruitful to consider the metaphors of the Khmer Rouge is in terms of how the signification of the metaphors may have changed over time. We can imagine, in general, a progression from "new" metaphor to "conventional" metaphor. The fact that the metaphors we are considering are readily pointed to by many Cambodians as innovations of the

Khmer Rouge and typical of the period is in itself an indication that they had not totally become conventional metaphors, although it is probably true that some of them had become conventional among the Khmer Rouge themselves. (It is interesting to see the Democratic Kampuchea period as a confrontation between people for whom certain metaphors had become conventional and people for whom they had not.)

The metaphors implied in the use of such words as *kâsang* and *lŭat dăm* were clearly originally intended to dignify what they referred to. It was only over time, when the original signification of the metaphor began to be lost and the actual use of the words became associated with the abuse of power, that the signification acquired irony and threat. The metaphor of *ângka* having the eyes of a pineapple is a different kind of metaphor, and it is harder to imagine its origins. But even this metaphor—which for us perhaps is difficult to disassociate from our own icons of threatening authority—may have been originally conceived in terms of benign power and only over time, by the ways it came to be used, acquired a suggestion of threat.

That these metaphors had meaning and power in the period is clear from the very fact that they were so widely used. But it is also clear that their usage was limited by an association with certain groups in certain power relations and that a large portion of the population felt some detachment from the world they suggested. One way of looking at the metaphors is as a deliberate attempt to mystify power relations; it is clear that if this was so it did not entirely succeed. I find it more interesting to think of them not so much in terms of a calculated attempt to mystify but as evidence of a conceptual framework within which the Khmer Rouge functioned—*part* of the purpose of which was to hide consciousness of power relations from the very people who were perpetuating them—a frame that related individuals to the state, drew on past conceptual systems, and was itself subject to change as the period evolved.

CHAPTER NINE

Gender Symbolism and Culture Change: Viewing the Virtuous Woman in the Khmer Story "Mea Yoeng"

Judy Ledgerwood

Khmer use literature to comment on their society in particular ways. Stories are often specifically didactic, telling people how to behave and providing models that demonstrate the good that comes to people who do good (*thvoe bŏn*) and the karmic consequences awaiting those who do bad (*thvoe bap*). In doing so, Khmer stories "tell" of a particular order in Khmer society which is both the telling of how society ideally should be ordered and how, in fact, at one time in the distant past society was organized. This chapter uses one Khmer story to illuminate Khmer conceptions of gender as a system of symbols, social order, and the process of culture change.

Anthropologists have long studied the power of symbols to condense, to summarize, to contain, and to convey various and even contradictory messages (see Turner 1967; Geertz 1973; Ortner 1973). Symbols becomes, in Turner's terms, "dynamic"; their multivalent nature endows them with certain generative properties (1967:20).

While recent work on gender in anthropology has discussed gender constructions as systems of symbols (see MacCormack and Strathern 1980; Ortner and Whitehead 1981; Collier and Yanagisako 1987; Strathern 1987), few works have focused specifically on culture change.[1] The issue of this connection between gender symbolism and culture change is particularly important because of the contradictory and paradoxical nature of gender symbolism.

As Kathryn S. March writes, "Gender symbolism is quintessentially mythic: . . . Gender not only provides multiple perspectives on the world, but those perspectives are interconnected, contradictory and simultaneous" (1983:741). Nancy Eberhardt agrees: "To study gender is inevitably to study paradox; researchers interested in cultural and social systems that distinguish and organize men's and women's lives are continually confronted with incongruities, ambiguities, and outright contradictions in patterns of belief and practice in image and reality" (1988:73).

By focusing on a single Khmer folk tale and how it is being retold and discussed as meaningful in various new contexts, this chapter draws out these contradictory aspects of a particular gender conception: the idea of the "perfectly virtuous woman" (*srey krŭap lĕakkh*).

The story is called "Mea Yoeng," "Our Uncle," but is also commonly known as "Srey kanhchoe thlŭh," "The Woman with Holes in Her Basket."[2] In summarized form, it goes approximately as follows:

> In the time of a compassionate and illustrious king, there lived in great misery a poor fisherman and his wife. The woman carried the fish her husband caught in a basket, but the basket was full of holes and many of the fish escaped. The woman was lazy and careless, and did not bother to repair the basket. One day a merchant vessel was passing along the river, and the wife of the chief of this vessel spied the fisherman's wife and called out to her, "Hey! Why don't you stop up the holes in your basket?"
>
> The merchant was angry at his wife, and also saw the remarkable beauty of the woman with the holes in her basket. He demanded that the fisherman exchange wives with him. His wife, being a *srey krŭap lĕakkh*, a perfectly virtuous woman, willingly followed her husband's orders; the woman with the holes in her basket was overjoyed at the prospect of being the rich man's wife and the poor fisherman was too afraid to object, so the switch occurred.
>
> The virtuous woman patched the basket and the catch increased significantly, so much so that she even suggested that he share some with their neighbors, who promptly decided the fisherman had a fine new wife.

The fisherman came home from chopping wood one day, and his wife recognized one particular type of precious wood. She had him find more, which she marketed, and they became wealthy. Then she suggested that her husband take up running, and when he became accomplished, she arranged to have him introduced to the king. When the king's horse ran at full gallop on an outing in the woods, only Mea Yoeng kept up with him. Alone in the forest, the king ate a wonderful meal prepared by Mea Yoeng's virtuous wife. Then on three different occasions, Mea Yoeng saved the life of the king and became his most valued servant.[3]

As for the new wife of the merchant, with her laziness and careless ways, she squandered away the wealth of the merchant. She had a baby by this chief of the boat. After the baby relieved himself, the virtueless woman wiped him with silk clothes, which she then threw away in the river. In time, all their wealth and the boat were lost, and they were reduced to begging from house to house. One day, they came to the home of their former spouses. The virtuous woman recognized them and pointed out that for their greed they now had nothing, while she who was tossed away had transformed a miserable person into a rich man. The couple were greatly ashamed, and left the mansion.

In setting out the activities of the two women, the story has much to teach us about how Khmer women are ideally to behave. They must know how to keep order in a household, how to cook delicious food, wash clothes, take care of babies. The virtuous woman is intelligent, advising and assisting her husband in his endeavors. The virtuous woman is beautiful, although in this story, as in many Khmer stories, both the virtuous and the virtueless women are beautiful.[4] The *srey krŭap lĕakkh* is generous, as is evidenced by the fact that she gives away part of her husband's catch.[5] She is also obedient, even to the point of leaving the boat wordlessly when so ordered by her husband.

Most important, the story focuses on the virtuous woman as keeper of the family's wealth. The virtueless woman is lacking particularly because the family fortune slips through her fingers; she allows the family's resources to be literally scattered behind her.[6] Wealth comes to the fisherman because his wife is careful with resources: first the fish, then the wood, which she knows how to price, transport, and market without being cheated. Further, she is able to recognize the hidden resources in the poor man and knows how to exploit them craftily for the benefit of the couple.

Because she possesses these various virtues, marks of high accumulations of merit from her previous lives, there is also a certain magical quality to the success of the couple.[7] Mea Yoeng is thus able to see and hear invisible spirits and defeat in battle a spirit in the form of a snake. In this story, the couple do work hard for their successes, but often in Khmer tales the virtue of the woman alone is sufficient to bring wealth to the family with no effort.[8] Her karmic status as confirmed by her proper behavior is sufficiently high that she and her spouse are rewarded in this lifetime.

Both men and women are ranked according to their karmic status within a single socioreligious hierarchy, and the virtues and vices of women can affect the status of men within this system. This perspective differs from the one commonly presented in studies of gender relations in Southeast Asia. Existing discussions, even some excellent ones, are almost always phrased in terms of the position of women in society versus the position of men (see Muecke 1981; Van Esterik 1982). This perspective follows the broader dualistic trend in gender studies within anthropology.[9]

More recently there has been a move within gender studies to study what Jane F. Collier and Sylvia J. Yanagisako (1987) call "culturally constructed social inequalities" or what Sherry Ortner and Harriet Whitehead (1981) call "prestige systems." They essentially discuss both men and women as hierarchically ranked within a single culturally constructed system of symbols. By viewing Khmer gender symbolism in this way, we can explain such phenomena as the relation between a queen and a male peasant or a rich merchant woman and a beggar. She can exist in this superior position because of her accumulation of merit.

A new collection of studies of gender systems in Southeast Asia edited by Eberhardt picks up this line of thought, focusing less on a single position of women and more on "understanding the processes and strategies by which gender systems themselves are created, sustained, manipulated and ultimately changed" (1988:6). One of the important results of such a shift, Eberhardt points out, is a renewed recognition of the "strong moral and evaluative flavor of gender ideologies" (6). Gender images and the expectations of behavior which they create are so compelling because of their "privileged position as part of society's moral order" (6).

While forming a part of the system of social order, gender conceptions retain their paradoxical nature. For example, A. Thomas Kirsch (1982, 1984) points out that Thai Buddhist gender conceptions associate women with economics, with "attachedness" in general, while men are associated more with withdrawal from the world and correspondingly with religious-political power. Men, who can be ordained as monks, have greater possibilities to earn merit. Charles F. Keyes (1984), however, focuses on the Thai woman as mother and on the merit earned when she "gives" her son to the religious order. Since, as Kirsch notes, the conceptions are relative, both views are correct, even though they are to an extent contradictory.

It is possible to state both that Khmer (and Thai) men are relatively more highly valued than women and to state that men and women are "relatively equal" (see Hanks and Hanks 1963:19; Ebihara 1968, 1974). A person's actual standing within society comes not from abstract rules but from a playing out of the various possibilities within parameters set by these rules and by the individual's circumstances. A listing of characteristics that affect one's meritorious standing, of which being male or female is one component, tells us little without further contextualizing information.

This complexity similarly is found within gender categories in discussions of ideal images, role models whose behavior one should emulate. These gender images, which provide models for proper behavior as polysemous symbolic constructions, offer different and often conflicting advice. So we find, for example, a critical characteristic of a *srey krŭap lĕakkh* is her soft-spokenness; in fact, her utter silence (she walks so quietly that you cannot hear the sound of her skirt rustling), and yet we find the merchant's wife yelling out, "Hey! why don't you fix the holes in your basket?" We find that a proper wife should never interfere in her husband's affairs, yet here we have a woman who seems to maneuver her husband throughout his various careers. A woman must be, as she is so often described in Khmer literature, *tŭan phlŭan, ph'aem lhaem*, soft and sweet; and yet in difficult situations, she must also be the hard-headed businesswoman, the woman maneuvering to get her husband "in" with the king, and a strong solid worker, even a fighter. All of these images are contained within the single symbolic idea, the *srey krŭap lĕakkh*. Like the notion that a man is always "bigger" (*thŭm cheang*) than a woman and the notion that men and women are relatively equal, which exist simultaneously in Khmer society, so too the proper woman is both silent and well-spoken.

This range of possible appropriate characterizations was present and no doubt useful in the relatively stable context of prerevolutionary Khmer culture. Different meanings could be emphasized by different individuals and groups in varying situations. As Victor Turner writes: "The symbol becomes associated with human interests, purposes, ends, and means, whether these are explicitly formulated or have to be inferred from the observed behavior. The structure and properties of a symbol become those of dynamic entity, at least within its appropriate context of action" (1967:20). But Khmer culture has experienced rapid and radical change. In the last twenty years, Khmer society has been tragically disrupted, and the Khmer today—in Cambodia, on the Thai border, and in the United States and other western countries—are critically concerned with "Khmerness," a concern that leads them to talk about and try to define the "moral order" of society. One way that they are doing this is by telling, republishing, and commenting on traditional stories, and their approaches provide insight into the process of culture change.

In a 1987 collection of folk tales published by the Ministry of Education in Phnom Penh, the story "Mea Yoeng" is reprinted. The story is essentially unchanged from earlier versions, but the volume includes an introduction that discusses the meaning of the stories in the new communist society. French-trained sociologist Vandy Kaon, the editor of this volume, writes:

> As for the story "Mea Yoeng," there are important moral lessons to be drawn. The ancients who told this story wanted to demonstrate that the young woman as wife has a very important role in that she sets the limits of her husband's destiny. The wife who is intelligent and of good character is the wife who is never negligent or frivolous and who knows how to assist and take care of her husband, work hard, and be motivated to search for successes in his life. Even if he

is poor, if he has a wife of good character, one who is honest, then his condition will steadily improve. But if, on the other hand, they are wealthy, this wealth can dissolve to nothing if the wife is a wasteful person, one who daydreams. Therefore, according to the wise ancients of our Cambodian society, women have a very important role. This is the reason that educating young women, teaching them to be of good character, to be virtuous, is important in Cambodian society. (1987b:9; my translation from the Khmer)

Although Khmer society has dramatically changed, not least in terms of demographics (there are now many more females than males in the adult population, and in some areas up to 70 percent are women [Boua 1981]), this message is remarkably unchanged from prerevolutionary Khmer literary commentary (see Ledgerwood 1990b). Kaon emphasizes the role of a woman as a loyal and trustworthy assistant, focusing especially on her role as the basis for financial stability.

While Kaon discusses the other tales in the Kaon volume at some length, he gives "Mea Yoeng" only this simple paragraph. In line with communist ideology and the constitution of the PRK government, which proclaims that women have equal rights with men, the general purpose of the section seems to be to say "women are important, too." This is new only in that it is being stated so directly, for the reasons that women are important—as pillars supporting their husbands' destinies and as keepers of the families' wealth—are traditional, emphasizing the ideal woman of the didactic codes (*Chbăp*): quiet, obedient, and good with finances.

The only part of Vandy Kaon's commentary that might be considered new is the last sentence calling for the education (*ka ăp rŭm*) of young women, if by this he means formal schooling. Young women usually quit school after primary school in prerevolutionary Cambodia (Cambodia, Ministry of Information 1965; Ledgerwood 1990b). It is extremely common for adult Khmer women to say that they were taken out of school because their parents feared that if they learned to read and write they would write love letters to boys. But *ăp rŭm* also means "to enculturate, to bring up (children), to train; education" (Headley 1977:1366), so Kaon could be referring here to the need to instill certain values, as well as the need for a classroom education in particular.

Meung Tholla, in a 1981 publication from Khao-I-Dang refugee camp titled *Vĭcchea ăp rŭm strey khmae* ("The science of raising girl children"), uses the same story in a strikingly different way.[10] She writes:

> The story "Mea Yoeng" shows the value of the intelligent woman, that is, the virtuous woman [*strey krŭap lĕakkh*], who is able to help educate her husband so he can change from being a mere fisherman to being a valued servant of the king. Because of the special talents of his wife, Mea Yoeng became successful in his life. This story demonstrates the power [*ĕthĭpol*] that women have over their husbands. That is, a virtueless woman [*srey khat lĕakkh*] can cause even the wealthiest boat owner to turn into a beggar, while the virtuous woman leads her husband to happiness and victory [*chôk chay*]. (1981:10; my translation from the Khmer).

Tholla's specific purpose in this section of the book is to encourage the education of girls in the sense of formal classroom training. While the message is the same, that is, the couple will prosper or decline financially because of the virtuousness of the woman, the key element in judging that value has shifted. Here, what is emphasized is the fact that the virtuous woman was educated, and because of this education she was able to help educate (*chuoy ăp rŭm*) her husband. It was she who saw to fix the basket, knew about precious woods, how to operate a business, and even what skill he should develop in order to properly serve the king.

Two words in particular betray a different tone to Meung's discussion. The first is the use of the term *ăp rŭm* to discuss the relationship between a wife and her husband. The term is usually used intergenerationally; that is, a teacher educates a student or a parent educates a child. To use it with reference to a woman seems to place her higher than her husband, whom she is educating. This idea is then stated clearly when the author writes that the idea of a woman educating her husband shows "the power (*ĕthĭpol*) that women have over their husbands."[11]

The message that a woman needs to educate her husband was also central to another version of the story I collected during my research. Here, this emphasis was even stronger, as though the husband were almost childlike. The female storyteller was a particularly important power broker in the American social service network.[12] Her husband, in contrast, was not active within the Khmer community. Her power derived from her employer, not from her marriage.

Her version also emphasizes, more than any other version does, the wrong enacted by the merchant when he sent away his virtuous wife. This female storyteller blames this act on the lust of the merchant. At the end of the story, as the impoverished couple leaves the house after coming to beg, this version stresses that now the man understands his guilt and knows that he had wronged his first, virtuous wife.

Two other male informants in the United States put no emphasis on education but rather, when talking of the virtues of the woman, spoke of such attributes as her ability to keep a clean house and her industriousness. One of their versions does include the fact that the wife of the merchant, who became the fisherman's new wife, had more education than he. This version ends quite differently, however. When the virtuous woman sees her former husband and his wife, she is embarrassed for them, calls them in, feeds them, and gives them money to start a new life.

All of the storytellers are telling the same story. All of them are telling a Khmer story and in so doing believe themselves to be passing on Khmer tradition. They all wanted to tell the story "correctly,"[13] for admitting to consciously changing the story would be unthinkable. The stories vary in the telling, yet the story tellers profess to changelessness. They see no contradiction, nor recognize any change occurring. Two aspects of this phenomenon are important. First, as a polysemous symbol in the range of Khmer gender conceptions, the ideal of the *srey krŭap lĕakkh* was always ambiguous and contradictory. She was, by definition, the quiet virgin and the screaming wife. She was the mother, both selfless and "attached." The range of options was always present—indeed, was "traditional."

But there is a second perspective on the way the stories are being retold and the uses to which the retellings are being put. Khmer in the camps, in western countries, and to a certain extent within Cambodia, are faced with a completely new range of circumstances. For example, one reason that girls were encouraged to go to school in the camps was that the surreal nature of camp life offered only one luxury: an abundance of free time. Another new phenomenon is the notion that a woman is a political patron in her own right because of the resources that she directly controls through the American social service network, rather than through her husband or father.

The stories are being used in these completely new situations, playing on the ambiguity inherent in the gender symbolism, to provide innovative solutions under the rubric of "tradition." Margie Nowak (1984) discusses this phenomenon with regard to refugees in general. The symbol, in Nowak's words, "accumulates connotations." In the extended liminal period that is refugee life, a dual process occurs: "The extended meaning of the term [symbol] is charged by its association with a powerfully evocative conventional understanding," and at the same time "the extensions of meaning suggested by the evolving metaphor add further import to the original signification." Thus, a term "gains in ambiguity as it becomes applied more innovatively to newer, broader referents" (162).

While Nowak is talking about key cultural symbols in general, I argue that this is particularly the case for gender symbolism, which is, by its very nature, paradoxical.[14] Khmer in different contexts use the story of Mea Yoeng to make the points that women are important in socialist countries, that young women should have education equal to men's, that men are childlike and in need of guidance and education, that what women really need is to know how to keep a house in order and handle the finances. A Khmer woman should be virtuous and thereby demonstrate a state of high merit so that she and her husband can benefit from it in this life. Through this proper behavior by women, society remains properly ordered. But in this time of social disorder, the manifestation of virtuousness is open to interpretation. The "play" in traditional conceptions of gender smoothes the transition to new types of order.

CHAPTER TEN

Sharing the Pain:
Critical Values and Behaviors
in Khmer Culture

John Marcucci

Clifford Geertz (1973) has claimed that human experiences are formulated into a "web of meaning" abstractly defined as culture. This chapter concerns the "web of meaning" the Khmer give to pain. The meanings of pain derive from sensate experiences recognized by complex cultural processes that contribute to and maintain ethnic identity. I explore critical values and behaviors related to pain which contribute to the persistence of, and processes within, Khmer culture. I propose that the cultural concept of pain, particularly the sharing of pain, is a major element by which the Khmer distinguish their identity and provide meaning to their existence. Indeed, the range and complexity of the meanings of pain span cosmological, biological, and chemical reactions. This perspective on pain, so suited to the generalist perspective of anthropology, has received scant attention, for most study is directed to the medicalization of pain, especially alleviating, controlling, and managing its perception and expression.

Mark Zborowski's (1952, 1969) and Irving Zola's (1966) early studies on the relation between ethnicity and the expression of pain support subsequent investigations finding "that an individual's ethnic background is a major determinant of how one communicates and expresses pain" (Lipton and Marback 1984:1279). James A. Lipton and Joseph J. Marback in their article "Ethnicity and the Pain Experience" (1984) suggest that future research in the sociocultural aspects of pain should focus on the meanings of pain for sufferers, that is, the concept of pain as a medical symptom and as part of the personal and social context of forming an illness reality (also Good and Good 1981).

Most important for this discussion, the concept of pain as a major element of culture extends beyond pain as a sign or symptom of illness. For the Khmer, pain reveals experiences of suffering and healing, and their act of sharing the experiences of pain continually contributes to the process of meaning.

Theravada Buddhism as practiced by the Khmer is a major belief system and it formulates the meaning of pain. The Four Noble Truths and the Eightfold Path might "mean little more than a general injunction to practice proper conduct" (Ebihara 1968:388–89), in the virtuous sense of attaining merit. Nevertheless, these Truths remain fundamental and central to the core belief of being Khmer, not from the idealized practice of the Eightfold Path, but through the experience of these Truths as the value of pain, namely suffering. Although Americans commonly view Buddhism as acceptance of or resignation to suffering, the spiritual power of Buddha does not cause suffering; the nature of life itself is the essence of suffering (Robinson and Johnson 1982).

Pain as a sensate experience is accorded critical values and meanings in Khmer culture. Judeo-Christian Americans may believe that pain is either given or taken away by God, and other American conceptions emphasize biological and chemical causes of pain and symptom alleviation. Generally speaking, Americans tend to separate beliefs into distinct and mutually exclusive categories: religious or scientific. Khmer also acknowledge the natural scientific aspects of pain and its alleviation, but such knowledge of "nature" is not separated from their cosmological world view based on Buddhism. The natural and spiritual aspects of pain are mutually inclusive for the Khmer.

Beyond Buddhism, another important part of Khmer cosmology is spiritism (or animism), a belief that magical spirits cause misfortune and affliction encourages people to take personal responsibility in coping with these problems. (Marcucci 1986:154). May M. Ebihara summarizes this aspect of Khmer religious syncretism: "Buddhism can explain the transcendental questions such as one's general existence in this life and the next. But the folk religion can give reasons for and means of coping with the more immediate and incidental, yet nonetheless pressing, problems and fortunes of one's existence" (1968:442).

In fact, it is the quotidian experiences of pain that provide individuals the ways for sharing pain through social interactions with others, particularly family members. Among the various means of socializing individuals to the group, Khmer medical practices offer a common, and often daily, means of providing a cultural context for the experience of pain.

Methodology

The study of pain requires a methodological approach that does not contrive the meaning and expression of pain, because meaning and behaviors vary and occur in different situations, and because the values assigned to beliefs about pain differ across cultures. Questionnaires and interviews, either open- or closed-ended measurement tools (Lipton and Marbach 1984), limit an understanding of the experience. Carolyn Sargent notes that among the Bariba of Benin and Nigeria "the subject of pain and the code of behavior surrounding painful experiences evokes from informants a cognitive map of honor and shame, rather than a discussion of pain *per se*" (1984:1299). Furthermore, as an observer of childbirths, Sargent recognized that "although there may be a paucity of verbal communication on the subject of pain, there is nonetheless a tacit dimension in the *shared understanding* of the experience of pain" (1301; emphasis added).

This chapter presents data I collected by participant observation among the Khmer in Dallas, Texas, during a six-year period from 1982 to 1987. I also visited the Khmer holding center in Thailand at the commencement of *chaul vossa*, when the monks retreat, in 1986.[1] Obviously the length of the research period facilitated an analysis dealing with process rather than classification. For example, the feeling of an acute pain might be treated by a medical practice that also inflicts acute pain, yet the behavioral reactions to these two sensations might be different. The value given to these experiences might emanate from the memory of painful events, some of which might be chronic, psychological, or historical. The approach to the study of pain as a cultural process is enhanced by the method of participant observation because the experience of pain remains within the "web of meaning" and is not removed from its social and cultural contexts. The following examples of the Khmer experience of pain are offered as a preliminary view that emphasizes the sharing of pain.

Afflictions of Suffering and Inflictions of Pain

I use the terms "affliction" and "infliction" to stress how closely related the experiences of pain can be, but differ regarding the meanings given within the context of the pain experience. Afflictions of suffering, in the sense I use it, describe conditions during which the endurance of pain becomes difficult and relief is usually sought. In contrast, inflictions of pain are sensations that are endured because of a perceived benefit or integration as a part of life.

Afflictions of suffering, caused by natural or supernatural disturbances, are manifested by various painful sensations, *chheu,* to the body and the psyche; this definition implies a holistic inclusion of both without the exclusion of body from mind. For example, a headache in Khmer is called *chheu kbal.* Often associated with this pain, *chheu,* is an emotional pain that expresses a conflict in terms of social and interpersonal relationships or stressful situations such as hard work, insufficient food, or extreme climatic conditions. A common affliction is the condition of "wind" or *khchăl,* which denotes an imbalance in the body. For the Khmer, "the causes of an illness are disturbances in their social and psychological, and biological environments . . . or from the malevolent actions of magical spirits" (Marcucci 1986:170).

Although French and other western pain medications, such as aspirin compounds, are known and used by the Khmer, the Khmer medical treatments of pinching, cupping, coining, and moxibustion (see Sargent, Marcucci, and Elliston 1983; Sargent and Marcucci 1984) are significant acts that contribute to the cultural processes of sharing the meaning of pain. "Pinching" involves literally squeezing the skin together until it becomes red. "Cupping" and "coining" obtain the same result by placing small cups over the skin or scraping the skin with a coin. "Moxibustion" involves putting a small amount of kapok (fibers from the ceiba tree) on the skin, on the forehead, for example, lighting it, then placing a small bottle over it. The vacuum created by the fire and the bottle creates a small reddish circle. These techniques are done to bring "dark" or unhealthy blood to the surface of the body. American providers of medical care to Khmer and other Southeast Asians have viewed these medical practices as forms of physical abuse (Yeatman et al. 1976), because the Khmer cultural conception of inflicting pain conflicts with American cultural values, which see pain only as suffering and as an experience that has only negative aspects and should be avoided.

C. Richard Chapman's review of biomedicine's current under-standing of pain and its management notes that "pain is one of the most complex human experiences. The sensory, emotional and mental aspects of pain are inextricably related and all contribute to pain behavior" (1984:1266). Nonetheless, for biomedicine in particular, and American culture in general, a major cultural con-ception is that pain represents a response based on "sensory mech-anisms . . . which detect and signal tissue injury"(1261). Certainly, an understanding of pain in terms of its values and behaviors crit-ical to cultural processes requires a comparative perspective that takes into account more than these signals and expressions (see Weisenberg 1975).

In numerous clinical encounters, biomedical practitioners voiced their amazement about the absence of expressions of pain among the Khmer. Exemplifying these cultural differences is the case of a Khmer man with shrapnel wounds. Over a five-month period he sought medical treatment for his hand, which was becoming dysfunctional, as well as for sites on his abdomen and groin. During a series of examinations, physicians deter-mined that his medical condition was not serious. They often re-marked about the patient's lack of pain because he did not grimace or yell out when they pressed and prodded his wounds. Fortu-nately, a rehabilitative massage therapist took great care to try not to cause much pain to the wounded areas, and he facilitated the increased functioning of this patient's hand and feeling of well-being.

The message therapy did of course inflict pain, but the context of its application imparted a sense of personal concern and a shared belief between therapist and patient that the pain of massage would facilitate the healing of the hand. Interestingly, although message is also a therapeutic practice in Khmer medicine, the direction of the massage practiced at this hospital ran toward the heart rather than away from it, causing the patient great concern. When the Khmer man explained the cultural meaning of the direction of massage relative to humoral and blood flows, the therapist made the appropriate accommodation, ensuring the patient's healthy improvement.

Carolyn Sargent and I, writing on Khmer obstetrical practices and the American clinical experience, noted that "Khmer response to pain drew the attention of some practitioners who observed that the women tended to be stoical and expressionless even during experiences which they themselves defined as painful" (1988:88). This was especially the case with regard to coining practices: "One nurse-practitioner, for example, commented that she was astonished the first time she saw marks of dermabrasion on a patient and was further surprised to learn that the woman's husband did it *for* her, and not *to* her" (88).

The differing values and behaviors of pain as a process are extremely pronounced in such cross-cultural medical encounters. Khmer medical practices inflict pain, but the context of meaning accorded that sensation is the benefit of healing and the restoration of harmony. The infliction of pain as a part of treatment not only restores humoral balances to the body, particularly the humor of "wind" but also communicates to others the status of the individual's affliction of suffering.

Treatments for the Cause of Affliction

The Khmer differentiate the degree of suffering not only by the type of affliction but by the type of treatment. For ordinary conditions of "wind," the practices of pinching, cupping, and coining are generally considered by the Khmer to be similar treatments that produce similar results, that is, the restoration of the humoral balance. Because "wind," however, is not the cause of affliction but the result, treatment is directed to the cause or causes, perhaps a constellation of social, psychological, supernatural, or magical circumstances. Treatment of the cause of the affliction is a critical behavior for the restoration of health.

The practice of pinching is a self-treatment whereby the individual inflicts pain by pinching locations on the brow between the eyes, the sides of the neck and, less frequently, the upper chest. This treatment leaves marks at the site of the application, and the Khmer recognize these marks as signs that a person suffers an affliction of pain. Usually a person interacting with the afflicted person does not confront the meaning of the treatment and affliction, as I often did, but rather responds in a caring and supportive manner. The offering of kindness and concern often helps the afflicted person discuss his or her troubles and conditions of pain. This social sharing of pain responds to one of the causes of pain, that is, social isolation or feeling the pain alone.

The treatment of pinching calls attention to one of the causes—a disturbance in social relationships. For example, a Khmer man in his twenties had a difficult time conducting marriage negotiations with the family of a woman he wished to marry. He frequently treated himself by pinching his brow between his eyes. When questioned about his treatment, he explained his condition of "wind." After I showed concern for his well-being, he stated that the cause of his affliction was a feeling of being in conflict with and isolated from both his family and his intended wife's family.

Another poignant illustration of pinching as a self-inflicted treatment that signals feelings of social isolation occurred when one of my close friends and informants reacted to my "un-Khmerness" by exposing the pinch marks on her neck and stating in exasperation, "khnhŏm chheu" (I hurt). The meaning of this pain was not that it was inflicted by the treatment; the affliction was suffering caused by the trauma of her emotional isolation.

In contrast, the treatments of cupping and coining usually require the individual to convey to others the nature of the affliction, at least in terms of "wind" and its effects. Those participating in this exchange will then decide the merits of coining or cupping, again based on a constellation of factors. As in pinching, the individual does not express pain during coining and cupping treatments because the value of pain is healing. The social context of cupping and coining is that they are ordinarily performed by a person who has a caring relationship with the afflicted person. Mother and father treat their children, spouses treat each other, and so on, with kinship dyads being the preferred social context for these treatments.

These treatments also serve to reinforce and strengthen social bonds. For example, a son sought treatment for his influenza symptoms by going to his mother's home and having her, rather than his wife, coin him. The coining was performed on a mat in the middle of the living room floor, with his parents and siblings giving him caring support. The family discussed not only his flu and "wind," but more important, the stressful situation of his working wife and his educational and employment expectations. As I reported elsewhere (Marcucci 1986), these medical practices are applied to children who are a year old; thus, the socialization process that communicates the behavior and value of sharing pain becomes a cultural process that is critical to group identity. The meanings of pain are derived from the group sharing the experience.

In addition to these behavioral characteristics, the Khmer also assign a value to the degree of suffering based on the subtle shades of color on the skin at the site of pinching, cupping, or coining treatments. Serious afflictions are denoted by deep shades, such as a purple color, that are described as *tŭm*, (ripe, or more mature). Other less serious conditions manifest themselves by treatment that results in lighter shades of color.

The treatments of pinching, cupping, and coining are usually self-applied or applied by family members. The afflictions may be minor or severe, acute or chronic, but healing occurs within the experience of the group when they share the pain.

Treatments by Specialists

Serious afflictions that are not healed by pinching, cupping, and coining sometimes require the care of a treatment specialist, or *krou* (see Ebihara 1968:433–43 for various types of healers). This healer has a broad variety of herbal and other medicinal concoctions and is thought to have special powers. One particular skill is the healer's ability to perform *phlŏm* or *phlŏm baley,* a blowing technique that can alter the humor of "wind." The healer blows "wind" over the afflicted person's body. On this "wind" are carried words in Pali, the scriptural language of Theravada Buddhism. One does not hear these words, but the healer and the afflicted person both share the belief that the "wind" carries the power of the healing words. For more serious afflictions, however, the effects of "wind" cannot counter the power of malevolent spirits. For this reason, treatment specialists or *krou* are often involved in other ritualized healing practices, such as moxibustion.

Moxibustion (*moxa,* or *ăt phloeng*) is a specialized treatment (see Marcucci 1986 for procedures). A *krou* inflicts pain on the afflicted person by burning kapok on the skin. The sign of having received moxibustion is permanent, for a scar forms at the place of treatment. Small children cry during this procedure, but adults receive it with no expression of pain.

I observed moxibustion treatment with several healers, and all provided a ritualized framework for discussing an afflicted person's concern about his or her well-being and the nature of the problems. Both the healer and the afflicted person offer chants, incense, and candles to the Buddha and the spirits. As the kapok pellet cauterizes the flesh, the healer performs *phlŏm baley,* blowing; its silent incantations fuel the burning pellet and provide an essential component of treatment, the spiritual meaning of suffering.

During the two years that my adopted uncle, Sem Sou, received moxibustion treatment, he received the power of his belief: the meaning of his affliction and the meaning of pain inflicted by healing. He gave numerous meanings to his illness during the two years of a complicated course of events, but the one meaning that could serve as a rubric is that of his ethnic identity emerging from conflict. This meaning was intertwined with past recollections of fighting to be Khmer and the present fight not to become blind.

In addition to Khmer medical treatment, he received western medical treatment for a serious hyperthyroid condition, Graves' disease. Among the various treatments, he took experimentally high dosages of the steroid Prednisone. He felt painful side effects from the high dosage, particularly severe Cushing's syndrome, but he believed in the value of pain as a process of healing.[2] His doctors were shocked by his tolerance level for pain, especially for the steroid side effects; but interestingly they verbally criticized his Khmer practices of cupping, coining, and moxibustion, calling them "barbaric." Nonetheless, in the face of this cultural conflict, Sem Sou practiced his beliefs and felt secure in his cultural identity. He knew that the cause of his affliction was inextricably related to the pain experienced by his people: *khmae*, the Khmer.

Similarly, Setha, a Khmer woman who had been afflicted with a swollen knee for more than ten years, shared the meaning of her pain by explaining that the cause of her misfortune is "hungry" spirits who remain insatiable because of the many Khmer who died during the war (Marcucci 1986).

Sharing Pain and Group Identity

The persistence of these Khmer meanings of pain and their associated cultural values and behaviors are being affected by adaptational processes experienced by Khmer groups living in the United States. In these social settings, American culture exerts its influence and mechanisms of social control, which contribute either to assimilation or to a perceived conflict that intensifies feelings of Khmer identity. Particularly in social contexts in which the Khmer seek services, such as American medical care, their adaptation to conforming behaviors lessens apparent cultural conflicts and facilitates interpersonal rapport. These situations by their very nature, however, constrain Khmer in expressing their own culture.

Individuals who go to work and school usually appear to conform to American customs. Some Khmer who live and work among Mexicans in Dallas learn Spanish, perceiving it as a trade language, and also adapt to Mexican customs. Indeed, contexts of cultural pluralism reflect not only how cultures influence one another but also how the relationship between cultures influences ethnic identity.

Yet one might speculate that the Khmer perception and ac-knowledgment of intercultural dynamics might be more discerning than those by American "melting pot" idealists, who perhaps per-ceive more assimilation than actually exists. Because in most Khmer households one or several individuals do not participate in the social activities of American culture, their medical practices tend not to be radically transformed. For the most part, the Khmer keep these practices private, in the family setting, and protect the identity of Khmer healers, *krou*. In so doing they maintain the in-tegrity of their medical practices, both in the value these practices place on pain and suffering and in the importance of participating and sharing in the experience of pain, suffering, and healing.

The tenacity and persistence of Khmer culture should not be un-derassessed because of observable traits and behaviors. The mean-ing of existence in the sense of group identity is intrinsic to the nature of that identify, which has been further intensified by war and refugee experience (Gonzalez and McCommon 1989), and it does not die easily. For example, in 1982, I examined Khmer Bud-dhist practices in Dallas and found not only an absence of formal Buddhist ceremonies, but that a majority of respondents affirmed Christian beliefs. My observations noted only a few remnants of Khmer Buddhism in the form of incense offerings at home. The Khmers' Christian pronouncements reinforced the ideas of assim-ilation as expressed by American sponsors. Yet the Khmer ob-served the Cambodian New Year by holding the proper Buddhist rituals secretly: they understood that Buddhism was not allowed in the United States.

One way of maintaining the meaningfulness of group identity is to protect that identity against intrusions from, and awareness of, other cultures. By excluding other cultural groups from participa-tion in certain behaviors considered critical to one's identity (e.g., medical practices), one might intensify the meanings assigned to such behaviors and contribute to their persistence. The Khmer in Dallas reveal the identity of indigenous healers only to trusted in-dividuals who will not compromise the integrity of meaning in the act of healing. And as more Khmer interact with Americans, they tend to hide the external signs of Khmer treatment, especially cupping on the forehead, by cupping parts of the body hidden by clothing. This secrecy and privacy seem antithetical to the need for group sharing in the experience of pain and suffering, a sharing that gives pain a significance of meaning and provides a certain resilience to the cultural process and persistence of the meaning of pain.

Conclusion

This essay attempts an understanding of Khmer meanings of pain which are critical to Khmer cultural process and persistence. The way the Khmer share their pain distinguishes values relating to suffering and healing. Critical behaviors in the social context of illness demonstrate how pain is endured as a part of healing. The Khmer believe that pain received during medical treatments is an infliction for healing, but this pain is only part of the experience. The restoration of health is dependent on treating the affliction—the perceived cause of pain. The Khmer demonstrate a capacity for cultural persistence by maintaining those values and behaviors that contribute to the healing of the individual and the group. Thus, an absence of behavior that expresses pain should not be misconstrued to mean that the Khmer are stoical or have a biological response to pain different from that of Americans. Nor should their expressions of pain be confused with somatization, a label often applied to patients of nonwestern cultures, which attributes emotional causes to physical distress. The Khmer teach us a particular cultural understanding of pain, suffering, and healing in their way of sharing beliefs and values.

CHAPTER ELEVEN

Cultural Consumption:
Cambodian Peasant Refugees
and Television in the "First World"

Frank Smith

Cambodian peasants relocated in the United States in the aftermath of the Khmer civil war (1970–75) and the murderous Pol Pot regime (1975–79) escaped the "killing fields" and have truly found a haven from the physical and social turmoil of that decade. The wholesale transplantation of these residents of the rural third world into the "postindustrial" urban United States is, however, in one sense simply the latest in a continuous stream of upheavals in Khmer peasants' lives.

These individuals had not been isolated from western culture and economy in the villages of Cambodia. But little could have prepared them for the myriad junctures and conflicts that necessarily occur when two such distinct entities as American culture and Khmer peasant culture—as that culture is both "instilled in" and lived by the peasants themselves—meet head-on. We can really understand this ongoing multifaceted process of intercultural interaction only by examining in detail its specific "nodes" or junctures. Moreover, these junctures form windows onto culture, or provide convenient points at which to examine the process of Khmer culture itself as it exists in America today.

This chapter examines in detail Cambodian peasant refugees' consumption of the popular entertainment medium of American television. I look at three substantive areas comprising this consumption: the persistence of Khmer spirit beliefs as they resonate with American fantasy epic films, the place of violent urban drama films in the refugees' understanding of their everyday lives in urban America, and the economic/cultural implications of the refugees' stated beliefs in the "reality" of televised drama in both these forms.

Cambodian culture, like contemporary American or any other culture, is constantly subject to accommodation, adaptation, and revision as it is practiced by the members of a society (Sahlins 1985:151–53). Therefore, although Cambodian peasants confronting everyday life (and, in this instance, television) in the United States come with a ready-made set of interpretive frameworks with which to make sense of the world around them, they are constantly rearranging and reinventing those frameworks and belief systems to deal with immediate events.

An important concept used in this chapter is that of "aesthetic disposition," defined by Pierce Bourdieu as "the only socially accepted 'right' way of approaching the objects socially designated as works of art" (1984:29). He uses the term aesthetic disposition to refer to the concept of taste as it exists in a culture; that is, the way the members of a culture "distinguish themselves by the distinctions they make." These distinctions extend well beyond the appreciation of art in the western tradition to the choice of entertainment styles, home furnishings, clothing, and everyday social practices (173).

In what follows, I briefly describe the context of my research. I then review some of the literature on television consumption and discuss some issues inherent in an analysis of third world/first world cultural interaction vis-à-vis television. Next, I outline some of the shared understandings brought by Khmer peasants to the reading of American television texts (e.g., traditions of performance consumption, culturally sanctioned belief systems). Finally, I describe the aesthetic and interpretative aspects of television consumption by Cambodian peasants in several refugee communities in the United States.

The Research

Most of the refugees in my study were from the Cambodian "rice bowl" province of Battambang.[1] These refugees came to the

United States with specific economic orientations, levels of formal educational knowledge, and aesthetic preferences or dispositions. The latter, a particular focus of my study, were evidenced in patterns of home decoration style, types of goods purchased, and modes of entertainment.

From the outset, these forms of "cultural capital" (Bourdieu 1984) distinguish Cambodian peasants from both mainstream white Americans and from their refugee counterparts of urban elite origin. The life choices proceeding from this cultural capital interact with structural factors in the American economic and cultural environment over time. In the process, the initial cultural and economic differences between Khmer peasant refugees and other sectors of American society are both maintained and widened.

My focus on television consumption was quite accidental and began after the discovery, early in my research, that the fantastic creatures in a *Star Wars* movie on cable television were in fact believed by a teenage refugee girl to be quite real. We were watching the movie together:

> *Soeun* [referring to the character "Yoda"]: "That little man's so funny."
> *Smith:* "Well, you know, that's just a puppet."
> *Soeun* [very suspiciously]: "He is? No, he's real, right? C'mon . . . that can't be a puppet . . . you're joking, right?"

From then on, when each new puppet or special effects creation appeared on the screen, Soeun and her sisters excitedly queried: "How about that one, Frank? That one's real, right? Look at that . . . that can't be a puppet!"

As I continued my observations and listened to refugees comment among themselves about programs seen on television, I soon became aware of how typical Soeun's perceptions of screen reality were. These observations enabled me to place Khmer peasant refugees conceptually within a specific class or aesthetic category of the American public and thus better understand their cultural/economic position in the United States and some of the means of its reproduction. In addition, I gained insight into the interaction of Khmer peasant beliefs concerning an unseen, supernatural world on the one hand (Marcus 1989) and their perceptions of the "concrete" and immediate goings-on of everyday life in America on the other.

Television Viewing, Reality, and the Third World

Many analysts of mass media's effects on the public emphasize a model of communications in which the electronic media, especially television, act upon and influence the world view and thus the behavior of a largely passive and ultrareceptive audience (Boddy 1983:7; Enzensberger 1986:96). In reaction to this concentration on the supposed effects of both television and film, others emphasize instead the role of audience members in an active construction of the meaning of mass media's messages (Williams 1975; Hall 1980; Wright and Huston 1981; Boddy 1983; Hodge and Tripp 1986; Lapsley and Westlake 1988). These analyses call attention to the interaction of media programs with individuals' life experiences—that is, how program content is interpreted by individuals in the spaces of its interaction with day-to-day social practice (Gardner 1985; Conquergood 1986; Hodge and Tripp 1986; Katz and Liebes 1987; Lapsley and Westlake 1988).

This approach mirrors a recent concern in anthropology with the ways that culturally received knowledge is reinterpreted and given new meanings by the individual as that knowledge intersects and resonates with everyday life experience (Sahlins 1982; Ortner 1984; Hefner 1985; Schieffelin 1985). This perspective in particular guides my analysis here. Specifically, I focus on the way Cambodian peasant refugees' individual and collective day-to-day social experiences and actions mediate (and are mediated by) their perceptions of the content—and, indeed, the "reality"—of American television.

Americans' views regarding the ways refugees and other third world immigrants to the United States consume culture—and these ways include third worlders' assumption of the "reality" or other misreadings of western media texts—have two manifestations.

The first of these is a somewhat smug humor about how third worlders are supposedly irresistibly drawn to and shaped by American media and other western cultural icons (Carpenter 1972; Fouquet 1981; McGinnis 1981; Kaye 1987). We are all familiar with jokes made in sitcoms, dramas, and talk shows, and in movies of all genres, concerning immigrants or other nonnative speakers of English falling all over themselves to acquire (and often "misuse") an American consumer good or cultural icon, or hopelessly misusing an English word or idiom. In the movie *The Gods Must Be Crazy,* such humor was the subject of an entire film. I argue that the underlying ethnographic message of such jokes amounts to "Well, it's no surprise that the rest of the world wants to be like us, and they'll do just about anything to achieve that goal, won't they?"

The second view is one of refugees and some immigrants as tragic, stoic relics of a "natural" and noble tradition (Kaplan 1989) who must somehow be protected from the ravages of the western media. As will become apparent later in this chapter, I am proposing a third view, one that acknowledges a greater agency on the part of social actors of third world cultures. That is, Cambodians' cultural consumption shows that they are neither blindly rushing to "become American" nor are they meticulously maintaining a nonwestern "cultural tradition." They are rather, as all social actors, striving to accommodate their cultural practices with social reality as they live it in the present.

Most analyses of the perceptions of television reality among westerners have concentrated on children's consumption of television, particularly as regards violence and racial and sexual stereotypes on the screen (Greenberg and Reeves 1976; Brown et al. 1979). W. James Potter (1986) has posited a continuum of reality perceptions of television programming among adults in the west. Stuart Hall (1980) has paid close attention to the role of viewers in the active "decoding" of the messages of television. This decoding process inevitably involves judgments about the "reality" or "falsity" of screen images. These writers (Newcomb 1987) emphasize the ways in which television might impart a specific world view to or influence the ideologies of viewers. Little attention (Carpenter 1972; Conquergood 1986; Bhargava 1987) has been paid to the phenomenon I observed among Cambodian peasant refugees: the ways viewers assume the concrete reality of what adult westerners know to be special effects or camera tricks.

There is an ongoing debate in anthropology as to whether or not outside observers can even impute a "reality" to a given entity (Sperber 1982).[2] Robert A. Levine (1984) and Paul Veyne (1988) insist that world views which posit the existence of mythic or supernatural entities must be judged on their own terms and within the contexts of their respective societies. These writers insist that one should not analyse myth using a rationalist, absolutist logic that has as its goal the specification of "actual" and "false," and "real" and "unreal"—a goal foreign to the logic of myth (Kapferer 1988).

There is also perhaps a tendency to label Khmer and other third worlders' perceptions of television and cinematic worlds as real as the result of cultural naiveté or a lack of education. The notion of television as laden with various codes and the fact that some individuals may not be able to interpret those codes properly (Wright and Huston 1981) also has relevance in the assessment of Cambodian peasants' understandings of television. One could simply point out that Khmer peasant refugees, unfamiliar with the magic of the camera, are reacting to television as the early audiences of Louis Lumière's films did when they ran from the theater at the on-screen sight of an arriving train (LaValley 1985). One could also stress the preconceptions Khmers bring to the viewing of television in the United States and point out how a preexisting view of the world—the structure of one's culture—shapes one's interpretations of new experiences (Maranda 1978).

Each of these approaches has a certain appeal, and many of the factors listed above are important in Khmer peasants' reactions to American television. After I outline what I see as Cambodian peasants' preconceptions concerning performance consumption and also concerning the world in general, I present evidence for my claim that it is first and foremost social experience that mediates the refugees' judgments about the content of television programming.

Cambodian Traditions of Performance Consumption

The realm of traditional Khmer dramatic performance is large and varied indeed. It includes masked dance (*lkhaon khaol*); a distinct form of operatic drama with both Indian and Chinese influences (*lkhaon basăk*); a number of different types of enactments of the Cambodian adaptation of the *Ramayana* (*Reamke*); male-female song duets (*ayai*) covering both religious and romantic/sexual comedic material; and a variety of epic poem and legends enacted on the stage (Brandon 1967; Huffman and Proum 1977; Pou 1983).[3]

David P. Chandler (1983) points to the didactic role of Khmer theater in the past, particularly that of the *Reamke*. Chandler and others writing about contemporary Cambodia and Southeast Asia in general detail the ways in which theater and dramatic art set forth themes that resonate with villagers' and urbanites' everyday lives and thus impart the tenets of cultural morality and link the supernatural and physical worlds in a deep and personal way (Huffman and Proum 1977; Schieffelin 1979; Chandler 1983).

Traditional Cambodian performance was and is far from uniform in its styles and in its effects on individuals across geographical and class lines; however, some generalities concerning not only Cambodian dramatic art but also Southeast Asian drama in general may be useful for the understanding of Cambodian peasants' ways of "consuming" performance. (I take all but the second of my categories from James R. Brandon [1967]).

1. Panoramic views of the unfolding of "larger than life" events are presented in traditional drama; that is, performances are comprised of many scenes and many characters and possess what Brandon (116) calls a "structural pattern of 'extension' " as opposed to western theatrical "psychological introspection."
2. A single performance work or style often contains many of what westerners might consider to be distinct forms of performance: comedy, religious epic, romantic drama, and so on.
3. Drama is often didactic. Relatedly, "good and evil are sharply defined and good must triumph over evil" (117).
4. Violence in drama is ubiquitous, explicit, and brutal.
5. Characters are strongly typed. (Brandon suggests six main types: gods, nobility, ascetics, clown servants, middle-class urbanites, peasants/laborers.)

Several of these general contours of traditional Southeast Asian/Cambodian drama are of interest in the study of peasant refugee consumption of performance media in the United States. The stress in traditional drama on "extension" and epic scale, the sharp definition of good and evil, the degree of violence, and the typing of characters (especially the figure of the hero) are in opposition to modern trends in contemporary western theater. Such elements, however, fit remarkably well with many of the elements in popular American science fiction and horror fantasy films such as *Star Wars, Aliens,* and *Friday the 13th,* as well as with adventure and crime-drama films such as the *Rambo* series or *Dirty Harry.*

Such contemporary American film conventions that fit well with traditional mythic and performance traditions (Hodge 1988) are also well-known markers of "popular" or "low" cultural performance in American society (Gans 1974). The consumption of such films serves as a ready-made cultural/aesthetic niche for Cambodian peasants as they arrive in the United States and, as we shall see, interact in interesting ways with their experiences in this country.[4]

The Setting: The Aesthetics of Television

The refugees had had limited exposure to television. Television sets were nonexistent in pre–Khmer Rouge village Cambodia. Indian and Chinese films dubbed in Khmer, Khmer productions patterned after the Indian model, and some western films had been available in the provincial capital of Battambang to the peasant refugees I studied. In addition, some western films as well as "propaganda" films made by the various countries that sponsored development projects in Cambodia (United States, Soviet Union, People's Republic of China) were shown from time to time on portable movie screens set up in rural areas. Informational health and hygiene films were shown in villages the same way (Mills 1968).[5] Movies were also seen on VCR-driven televisions and projected on large screens in the better-equipped refugee camps in Thailand and the Philippines. These showings featured much American fare.

Cambodian refugees in the United States have physical access and the cash to purchase television sets. They are thus rapidly transported to the private ownership level of television-viewing which most societies have reached over time and through a number of transitional phases between public and private viewing (Bogart 1956). Television sets were present in virtually every refugee home I visited in Wisconsin and Illinois. Of these sets, all had color, 90 percent had cable service, and over 50 percent were linked to VCRs. Nearly all Cambodian peasant refugees live on low, fixed incomes, but television sets and VCRs are often one of the first items purchased by a family.[6]

In the home, the TV is a centerpiece. The set is often adorned with colorful plastic garlands, family pictures, and a variety of plastic toys and statues. The table on which the set is placed usually holds a *manhe* (from French *magnét*, meaning "portable stereo") as well, and is surrounded by Buddhist posters and Hindu drawings of the gods Krishna and Radha (see Smith 1989). Pictures of Thai classical dancers, promotional calenders from local Asian markets, posters of Chinese movie stars, and posters of Angkor Wat and/or Thai and Burmese temples also adorn the walls around the TV. The overall effect is not only a colorful center of attention in an otherwise sparsely decorated living room but also what I would call an aesthetic showcase.[7]

The television set is almost always left on, although the sound is often turned down while Cambodian traditional popular music blares from the "boom box." Cambodian peasant homes are almost never devoid of loud and animated human activity, and conversation, laughing, and arguments continue almost nonstop while the television is on. Usually, however, someone in the home—adult or child—pays fairly close attention to the set at any given time.

When a group of Cambodian refugees are actively watching a program, they engage in a continual dialogue of observations, interpretations, and questions. Few peasant refugees over the age of twenty-five understand English well, so some of this conversation is a group attempt to translate the dialogue of a program. Even when dialogue is understood—and it is usually readily understood by children—constant debates can be heard about the meaning and significance of program content (Katz and Liebes 1987). These debates may concern the degree of relevance of the program to the refugees' lives or its parallels in traditional Cambodian drama:

> *Rim,* a fifty-five-year old woman (watching a Western): "Hey, this story's just like something they would perform in *yike* [a form of Khmer dramatic performance]."
> *Pon,* a fifty-year old man: "No, no, no! You're crazy. They would never do that in *yike*...maybe in *lkhaon basăk.*"

Debates over specific traditional performance styles and "codes" and their meaning (Brandon 1967) also occur when films dubbed in Khmer, Khmer films, or tapes of Khmer traditional dances are watched.

A concept of actors (*tuo aek*) and of the enactment and representations of historical events (*ke dămnael*) certainly exists in Cambodian peasants' view of performance, but there is much confusion over whether a film—particularly a Western—is a staged representation of history or whether it is an actual filmed document. This is precisely the subject of many debates and of the questions refugees asked me concerning television content (see also Conquergood 1986).

> *Yann,* a forty-three-year old man, watching the 1977 film *Day of the Animals,* in which a woman is attacked by eagles: "Frank, is it real?"
> *Smith:* "No, it's a trick done with cameras and models of birds. . . . They aren't real birds."
> *Yann,* whose tone indicated he is not sure I know what I am talking about: "But . . . look . . . we can see the birds' beaks peck and hit her flesh, *pok, pok, pok,* and the blood. . . . How would they do something like that, Frank?"

Another possible, slightly more skeptical interpretation of Yann's comments might be that he does not really believe the effects are real, but rather that he is actively struggling to make sense of the strange new culture (American) he sees represented on the screen by politely asking for explanation by a member of that culture (myself).

My recorded observations and analyses that follow are intended to explain just why certain programs come to be perceived as real. First I describe the two main types of films viewed on TV by the refugees—videocassettes of movies of Asian origin and American films and serials—and then concentrate my analysis on the latter.

Indian films have long been popular among the peoples of Southeast Asia; Cambodians are no exception. These films are filled with spectacular fight scenes, slapstick comic escapades, and numerous lively love songs and dance numbers. In the Indian fantasy epics based on the *Ramayana* and other classical Indian literature, portrayals of supernatural creatures with various special effects are also common.[8] These films have been dubbed in the Khmer language and can be rented today in Chicago or borrowed and copied from friends and relatives. Thai films are also common fare, as are Chinese martial arts serials.[9]

Pre-1975 Khmer films are highly valued by the refugees, but the few copies that circulate are of extremely poor quality and are fast deteriorating. There is, however, a thriving Khmer film industry in California, Texas, and other areas. One of the popular offerings of this industry is extended vignettes (often closely patterned after American music videos) of Khmer life in the United States set to Khmer pop songs, as well as somewhat idyllic reenactments of prewar village life accompanied by traditional folk music. In addition, film records of traditional Khmer court and folk dancing widely circulate via videocassettes. These tapes are made chiefly in the United States, France, and Cambodia.

The special effects in the fantasy and adventure movies mentioned above would doubtless be mocked as hopelessly amateurish by western consumers of "state-of-the-art" American-produced special effects showcases. Khmer peasants, however, do not criticize such films in this way, even when comparing them with American-made fantasy films. Many of the peasant refugees I spent time with also do not believe that the Indian, Chinese, and Thai films they watch have been dubbed into the Khmer language. I would often hear comments such as: "You know, this is an Indian movie, but the people in it speak Khmer," or "See those Chinese people in that movie? They know how to speak Khmer. Actors are very smart and can often speak many languages." Others, however—and the distinction can usually be made along class lines— simply point out: "Oh, they've added Khmer voices to that film [*bânhchaul sǎmleng khmae*]."[10]

Images of Fantasy

Much of the American television watched by peasant refugees is comprised of fantasy, horror, and science fiction films. These are seen on HBO and other cable channels. As I mentioned earlier in a discussion of a teenage girl's perceptions of a *Star Wars* movie, the lightning-bolt wielding or flying humans, grotesque demons, and talking animals of western (as well as Asian) fantasy films and television programs are perceived by many refugees to be pictures of real persons and things. Besides *Star Wars, Alien, Ghostbusters,* reruns of the television series *"V", Enemy Mine, E.T.,* and *Halloween* are all favorites of peasant refugees (Conquergood 1986).

Other types of films, such as the *Rambo* movies, Chuck Norris films, "Dirty Harry"–type urban vigilante dramas, *Lethal Weapon, Commando,* and war movies such as *Platoon* or HBO Vietnam War vignettes are also favorite fare for the refugees. Peasant refugee men and women watch programs such as nationally televised boxing matches (a particular favorite is anything featuring *taysun* [Mike Tyson]) and "World Wrestling Federation" broadcasts for hours on end, exclaiming and interjecting wildly throughout. In these movies and programs, most scenes of violent death, serious injury, and spectacular explosions in which large amounts of property and life are lost are also taken as film records of actual events.

Cambodians pay a great deal of careful attention to these violent films. Every time someone is ripped apart by machine-gun fire, thrown through a window, or karate-kicked to the head, one of the refugees will invariably supply a verbal description of what just happened. Arguments are common over just how serious an injury has been sustained in a given incident and over whether or not the victim is dead yet:

> *Kin,* a fourteen-year-old male, watching a martial arts fight scene: "Oh, he's gonna kill her . . . Ugh! Damn! . . . Oh, she's dead. She's dead already."
>
> *Toeun,* a twenty-two-year-old male, watching a martial arts fight scene: "Oh, he's dead. Watch, watch . . . *pung* [a sound effect]! Shit! That's it. He's gonna die for sure. Look . . . there's the blood. Oh, he's dead for sure."

In addition, various American dramas, comedies, and teen "sex-ploitation" films are quite popular. The main draw of these films seems to be their representations of what peasant refugees see as the bizarre and very foreign behavior of Americans. These programs are the source of endless amusement and fascination for refugees, providing them with a means for scrutinizing Americans in what appear to be their "normal," day-to-day activities without the uncomfortable necessity of face-to-face interaction. Particularly fascinating to peasant Cambodians are what they see as the loose sexual mores of Americans and the high incidence of nudity displayed on the screen.[11]

Finally, I should mention the 1984 film *The Killing Fields*, which is highly valued by most Cambodians as a largely accurate record of their experiences under the Khmer Rouge. They watch this movie over and over again, both on cable television and on videocassette, constantly discussing it, analyzing it, and arguing over its fine historical points. So much do they perceive this film as an accurate record of the Pol Pot years that many peasant refugees believe that it was actually filmed in Cambodia while the Khmer Rouge ruled. Many believe that the depictions of forced labor and killings in the film actually occurred, but individual interpretation varies according to personal experience. For example, Lai, a twenty-six-year-old woman, motioned excitedly toward the screen at the point in the film where a young child and one of Dith Pran's fellow escapees are killed by a land mine: "See that? That's not real—they staged that. But before, when the Khmer Rouge smothered that man with a plastic bag? Boy, that was real. . . . I've seen that."

I now turn to a detailed analysis of two of the major types of American television/film consumption by peasant refugees: fantasy epics and urban crime dramas.

Screen Representations of the Spirit World

The world of the supernatural looms large in the world view of the Khmer peasant. Many believe that animistic spirits and Buddhist deities play a part in virtually every aspect of social and material existence (Delvert 1961; Thierry 1985; Ang Chouléan

1986; Porée-Maspero 1962–69). Khmer village life can in many ways be seen as a constant series of accommodations and supplications to, and avoidances of, the benign and malevolent supernatural creatures that inhabit the forest, guard the home, bring good fortune, and lie in wait in times of sickness (Thierry 1985). It can be argued that the requirements of the spirit world in Cambodia, together with the moral precepts centered on activities in the village Buddhist temple, form the organizing force of rural social life (Ebihara 1968).

It is not enough to say, however, that "because Khmers believe in the supernatural, they accept representations of the supernatural on television as real." I would rather point to the legitimating and reinforcing effect that watching *Star Wars, Big Trouble in Little China,* or *Friday the 13th* has on the perceived reality of the spirit world in everyday life. Virtually every Cambodian peasant has, at least one story of a personal encounter with the supernatural. These stories range from older Khmers' eyewitness accounts of deaths caused by evil magicians to the reports of ghosts seen by young and old alike. Such events are said to have taken place in Cambodia, the Thai refugee camps, or here in the United States.

These supernatural encounters are so widely distributed and consistent among Khmers because they are culturally defined as real and appropriate, although by this I do not mean that Cambodians do not truly believe they have experienced such phenomena—they certainly do. Many of the more spectacular, "concrete" encounters with the spirit world so prominent in Cambodian discourse, however, are the stuff of legends, passed down over time and reported second- or thirdhand. It is precisely this type of encounter with the supernatural—vivid, spectacular, and unmistakably "real"—which appears to Cambodians living in the United States to have been captured on film. The producers of fantasy films with supernatural themes (or science fiction films perceived by the refugees to have supernatural themes) thus unknowingly enter the very same space in which Cambodian spirit belief exists.[12]

Television is a medium controlled by those whom Cambodians see as technologically advanced and of superior abilities in many areas: that is, westerners. Peasant refugees believe that those who film the "events" they see on TV have used their cameras to record

on film what Khmers know was there all along: the world of spirits, clearly defined and in living color, as it were. The spirits they
see on the screen, which may make their own ongoing day-to-day
encounters with spirits pale by comparison, nevertheless are in
form and function in full agreement with those experiences:

> Yann, watching Big Trouble in Little China: "See all those powers
> they have . . . all those spirits they control . . . how they can crip-
> ple someone just by raising their hands? In Cambodia, it's just
> like that. . . . Oh, Frank, you can't imagine the powers some
> Cambodian magicians [thmŭap] have!"
> Darann, a thirty-eight-year-old woman, watching a fireball fly
> through the air in Darby O'Gill and the Little People: "Oh! You
> see that? We used to see that same kind of spirit in Cambodia,
> shooting through the air at night. You have them here, too. . . .
> I've seen them right out in back of the apartment building, by
> our gardens."

Yann's comments here, as his earlier observations on the reality of
special effects, could alternatively be interpreted as a polite attempt to draw some parallels between Cambodian and American
culture.

Images of Urban Violence

The Cambodian peasant view of Americans as intelligent and
powerful beings applies to the refugees' perceptions of urban vigilante films as well. It is of no small significance to Khmer peasants
that the victors and enforcers of moral order in these films are
white males who end up out-thinking (and often violently murder-
ing) their obviously immoral, evil, and often nonwhite opponents.

The Cambodian aesthetic preference for light skin, even among
many dark-skinned peasants, is well known to all acquainted with
Khmers (Becker 1986; Criddle and Mam 1987; Smith 1989). This
preference apparently predates contact with Europeans and is no
doubt related to the economic success of the (light-skinned) Chinese in Cambodia and to the practical advantages of acquiring a
Chinese husband (Steinberg et al. 1959).

A related, long-standing association of dark skin with moral in-
feriority and poverty is reinforced in the refugees' world view
when they arrive in the United States. Cambodian peasant refugees
have almost invariably settled in poor, primarily black urban
neighborhoods in this country; they are often the victims of crime,
and the refugees see blacks as the most visible perpetrators of these
crimes. The refugees assume that blacks, as the primary inhabitants of the dilapidated urban neighborhoods in which they must
also live, are responsible for the physical and economic condition
of these neighborhoods. Many refugees consider blacks to be immoral, dangerous, and in general the "problem group" of American society, a foil to what they see as the "moral superiority" of the
Khmers' benefactors, middle- and upper-class white Americans.[13]

In the urban vigilante movies such as the Dirty Harry series
mentioned above, blacks are often portrayed as a group of wild,
dangerous criminals in need of control (Berry 1980; Woll and
Miller 1987). These images of blacks resonate with the refugees'
own experiences, which have already been interpreted within a
prejudiced framework:

> Bol, forty-five, watching blacks beat up a white man: "Oh, the
> blacks in Chicago are just like that, Frank—they're really evil
> people. When I would walk to the store, they would push me
> around and throw dirt in my face. . . . They took my money, too.
> They're worthless, evil people . . . just like those guys beating up
> that man. . . . Why are they like that?"

An image of whites as powerful and moral is reinforced simultaneously as peasant refugees watch the films, every time a muscular
urban vigilante "blows away" another evil criminal.

The refugees' perceptual link with the bloody violence and spectacular pyrotechnics of war films such as *Platoon* and programs
like *Tour of Duty* is also one of social experience. Watching people, often family members, tortured by the Khmer Rouge or blown
apart by mines is an all-too-familiar experience for Cambodians
who lived through the violent Khmer civil war and the Khmer
Rouge rule that followed. In one sense, seeing these events reen-
acted on the screen—and at times, varying from individual to in-

dividual, they *are* perceived as reenactments—has a cathartic effect on Cambodians.

Most often, such events are indeed assumed to be real. Such depictions of violence are certainly no more remarkable than those Cambodian peasants have heard told in legend and folk tale since birth or seen with their own eyes. In general, movies about the Vietnam War (as opposed to, say, depictions of violence in the Middle East or South Africa) are the types of war films most often perceived as being actual records of events, probably because of the relevancy of the former films' setting to Cambodians' own experience:

> Bol, fifty-two, watching *Tour of Duty:* "Have you seen this before? These are pictures of the war between the United States and Vietnam. . . . See those palm trees, and the rice fields? That's Vietnam; that's Asia. My country's not so different."

For Cambodian peasant refugees, television is an important form of entertainment which also resonates with their life experience. This resonance occurs in the "historical" context of the belief in the spirit realm and the world of the traditional supernatural epic so important to the Khmer peasant world view and identity. It also occurs in an everyday, contemporary context as regards somewhat infrequent encounters with spirits in the United States and, to a larger degree, encounters with the violence and turmoil that are part of life in urban, poor America. In the larger context of American culture, Cambodian peasants' consumption of television is but one instance of the insertion of the Khmer into a mosaic of disadvantaged ethnic underclasses in America.[14]

Cambodian peasant refugees constitute yet another addition to the waves of third world residents entering the United States, people impacted by and entangled in American economic and cultural production worldwide.[15] The cultural aspects of American/third world relations, only one element of a larger picture, play an important role in maintaining, or reproducing, these relations.

Paul DiMaggio argues that among the middle class in American society, improved communications and other factors have considerably loosened the boundaries of taste cultures (or patterns of aesthetic disposition) or "status cultures" (1987), so that there is a wider acceptance of other cultures. For disadvantaged social and economic groups in the United States today, however, such divisions are as strong as they ever were. This is as true for Cambodian peasants in the United States as it is for the American black underclass, situated as they both are in similar ethnic/economic/social categories (Bach 1986).

This is not to say that Cambodian peasants are maintained in a disadvantaged economic position in American society because they watch "kung fu" movies, "B" slasher movies, and professional wrestling and believe that most of the events portrayed in these programs are real. It is not the viewing of such media, or simply refugees' perceptions of the media, which accomplishes such a formidable task. But one highly visible element of Khmer peasant refugees' *reproduced* disadvantaged position in this country is without a doubt their patterns of cultural consumption and aesthetic dispositions, none of which can be said to exist independently of Cambodian peasant refugees' economic position. As one scholar points out: "The presentation which individuals and groups inevitably project through their practices and properties is an integral part of social reality. A class is defined as much by its *being-perceived* as by its *being,* by its consumption—which need not be conspicuous in order to be symbolic—as much as by its position in the relations of production" (Bourdieu 1984:483).

What is significant is that these patterns of consumption are in many ways shared with the other disadvantaged ethnic and social groups with which Khmer peasant refugees share their neighborhoods and apartment buildings, the very groups that are, unfortunately, counterposed with Cambodian refugees in sets of often violent, extremely antagonistic relations (Ebihara 1985).

This perspective is just one, I argue, that we should begin to use to look at Khmer peasant refugees—as a distinctive group of displaced Southeast Asians with a history, to be sure—but also as yet another element in a growing American mosaic of socially and economically disadvantaged ethnic groups, set apart from white America by skin color, income, and cultural consumption, negotiating their way through the world in daily social practice and

changing the "structure" of their collective selves in the process—
and getting more and more distant from "mainstream" America
every day.

What the refugees are not is a precious though tragic artifact,
possessors of a culture that is somehow frozen in time, woefully
out of place, and the sole determinant of their every perception and
action in this country. Cambodian refugees are participants in a
contemporary Cambodian culture, which, for over two hundred
thousand Khmer, is now and forever intertwined with the social
and cultural fabric of the urban first world.

Notes

1. Introduction

1. The Sociology Institute still exists in name at the time of this writing (March 1993), but it did not seem to function as a research organization after Vandy Kaon, the former director, had left the country in 1989.

2. The name Pol Pot itself has come to stand for the regime he headed in the second half of the 1970s.

3. This number fluctuated.

4. There is an equation here between Khmer and Cambodian, but "Cambodian" in the sense of nationality includes Chinese, Chams, and other groups.

2. Khmer Literature since 1975

1. See *Tossânavâddey Roupheap*, illustrated journal published between 1975 and 1979.

2. See *Tossânavâddey Roupheap*, December 1976:10–11.

3. See a 45-speed record titled "17 Mésa Moha Chôk Chay, Glorieux 17 Avril, Hymne National du Kampuchéa Démocratique, Vincennes, n.d. (sold during the annual French communist "L'Humanité" festival in 1976).

4. See a 45-speed record titled "Chants révolutionnaires du FUNK [United National Front of Kampuchea]," Vincennes, n.d. (sold during the annual French communist "L'Humanité" festival in 1976).

5. This was the case for Pok Ponn So Mach (1988).

6. Interview conducted with Chheng Phon by Natalia Fochko, researcher at the Academy of Sciences in Moscow, in 1988 (unpublished original text in French).

3. Khmer Traditional Music Today

1. Judy Ledgerwood, "Changing Khmer Conceptions of Gender: Women, Stories, and the Social Order," Ph.D. diss. (Cornell University, 1990b), mentions that they were available under the counter in the markets of Phnom Penh.

4. The Revival of Masked Theater, *Lkhaon Khaol*

1. Where the common spelling of a temple name is different from our transliteration, the transliteration is provided in parentheses the first time the name occurs. This is also true for the word "wat," temple, itself, which we transliterate "vat." It is left as wat in these titles for the convenience of those who know that spelling.

5. Cambodian Buddhist Monasteries in Paris

This paper is based on research supported by the Royal Geographical Society, the International Federation of University Women (1965–66), and the University of Durham (1984–88). I am grateful for this assistance.

1. The Venerable Yos Huot left his position with the United Nations Border Relief Organization in 1990 and now travels widely, working for peace and aid for Cambodia. He has visited Cambodia several times since then.

2. For monks: *Sattaparitta-Dvadasaparitta* (1965), and for lay people: *Gihivinaya Samkhepa* (1963).

6. Khmer Buddhists in the United States

1. I personalize the name "Pol Pot" as Khmer do, as a symbol of all the evil that has happened to them.

2. Christians in Cambodia before 1970 numbered only in the hundreds.

3. "Bounthan" is a pseudonym, as are all informants' names in this chapter. The data come from Judy Ledgerwood (unpublished field notes, 1988).

4. "Crossing the river" means to have a baby, but is also a metaphor used for discussing spiritual salvation. See Hansen (1988).

5. Ledgerwood and I witnessed a religious healing in a Chicago *vât* in 1983.

6. The Tamil referred to in the Sri Lankan prophesies.

7. David P. Chandler (1991) says that he has heard similar comments from refugees who have not heard of Pŭtth's writings.

8. This metaphor is frequently cited by Khmer refugees.

9. See Chandler's translation and discussion of this story: "Songs at the Edge of the Forest" (1982:53–77).

7. Khmer Proverbs

1. For more discussion on poetic devices see Abrahams (1972: esp. 119–21).

2. Two collections of proverbs in French are available: Pannetier (1915) and Finot (1904).

3. See Huffman and Proum (1977:143–48) for a brief introduction and extract from the Kotĭlôk.

4. See Huffman and Proum (1977:167–72) for an extract.

5. Several of these folk tales can be found in their entirety in Huffman (1972).

6. Some informants consider sayings and predictions of the Buddha to be a distinct type of expression, not to be grouped with proverbs. Such expressions are not consistently labeled as Buddhist in origin by all informants: therefore I leave the discussion of distinguishing them to future studies.

7. One available primer in which a proverb is seen in the first reading is United Nations High Commissioner for Refugees (UNHCR) (1980:72). An example of a novel in which proverbs appear frequently is Sŏphat by Rim Kin, reprinted in its entirety in Huffman (1972). A methodology for analyzing proverbs can be found in Tau Hing (1955).

8. Examples are Sŏk Sâbay magazine, published in Khao I Dang by the International Rescue Committee (1985), and proverbs painted on the interior of the Neighborhood 7 food-distribution center in the Philippine Refugee Processing Center in Morong, Bataan.

9. The folk tale is in Huffman (1972:29–33). The proverb can also be found in Chbăp Pĕak Chăs, in Huffman and Proum (1977:168).

10. The folk tale is reprinted in Huffman (1972:67–69).

11. This proverb is used in the novel Sŏphat reprinted in Huffman (1972:298).

12. This folk tale is reprinted in Huffman (1972:11–15).

13. This proverb occurs at the end of the folk tale about Alev reprinted in Huffman (1972:141–88).

14. Both proverbs are found in the Chbăp Pĕak Chăs reprinted in Huffman and Proum (1977:168).

15. The earliest written attestation I have found of this proverb is in Pannetier (1915:54). A contemporary interpretation of this proverb is noted in the introduction to this volume. Many Khmer have also told me that this proverb is really a prediction of the Buddha; thus they believe that the upheaval during the Khmer Rouge years was foreseen by the Buddha; see Frank Smith (1989).

16. This proverb is seen in a folk tale found in Huffman (1972:55–60).

17. These images and others found in proverbs are discussed in Thierry (1958: esp. p. 443).

8. Metaphors of the Khmer Rouge

This chapter is based on research funded by the Indochina Studies Program, a subcommittee of the Joint Committee on Southeast Asia of the Social Science Research Council and the American Council of Learned Societies. My thanks to the many people who have helped me with this project, especially to my coresearcher, Sotheary Duong, and to many other Cambodian friends and informants.

1. Cambodian refugees have sometimes identified the figure to me inaccurately as Prohm, or Brahma. We find this identification in United Nations High Commissioner for Refugees (UNHCR) textbooks used in refugee camps: *Rien Âksâ Khmae Thnăk* (Beginning Khmer reader) 1, 2, 3, 4 (1980, 1981a, 1981b, 1981c), which seem to be based on earlier Cambodian textbooks.

2. Refugees tell of couples swearing to *btechnha* as part of their wedding ceremonies.

9. Gender Symbolism and Culture Change

Research for this work was assisted by a grant from the Indochina Studies Program of the Joint Committee for Southeast Asia of the Social Science Research Council and the American Council of Learned Societies with funds provided by the National Endowment for the Humanities, the Ford Foundation, and the Henry Luce Foundation. I am most grateful for this support.

1. An exception is Sylvia J. Yanagisako (1987) who explores ideas of kinship and gender among two generations of Japanese Americans.

2. This story was the one that came to people's minds most often during my research on Khmer stories and ideal images of women. This project involved a year of research in five American cities in which I interviewed Khmer and searched for storytellers. For collected versions of this story, see Judy Ledgerwood tapes KG-JL-A008, 009, and 014, which are stored at the Indochina Archive at the Library of Congress (1989). Published versions of Mea Yoeng include the version in the *Brâchŭm Reuang Préng Khmae* published by the Buddhist Institute and another version for use as a textbook. These two versions, both in poetry, vary slightly.

For commentary on the story, see Thierry (1978); Khing Hoc Dy (1977); Vandy Kaon (1987b); and Meung Tholla (1981).

3. Fuller versions of this story expand on each of these three episodes.

4. On the beauty of women in Khmer literature, see Khing Hoc Dy (1980:45–68).

5. This episode of the story was not mentioned in the oral versions I collected, although each storyteller noted qualities that demonstrated her virtue in other ways.

6. The wording here is very similar to warnings for women on losing the family's wealth found in the didactic codes for women, the *Chbăp srey;* see *Chbăp brŏh, Chbăp srey* (Didactic codes for men and women; 1959). For a more complete discussion of the importance of the didactic codes for women, their different versions, and mode of transmission, see Ledgerwood (1990b).

7. On *lĕakkh* as "marks" and on *srey krŭap lĕakkh* in general, see Khing Hoc Dy (1977).

8. See, for example, the following stories: "Bŏrâs kămchĭl mean brâpŭan krŭap lĕakkh" (The lazy man who had a perfect wife; 1971), and "Sâmlănh pi nĕak" (The two friends; n.d.).

9. See, for example, the distinctions "nature-culture" made by Ortner (1974:67–68) and "domestic-public" made by Rosaldo (1974).

10. According to employees at the same printshop in 1989, the book was actually written by two people, Meung Tholla and Meung Phalla, a man about forty years of age and a woman in her late thirties in 1981. Both had been teachers, one at Lycée Sisowath in Phnom Penh and the other at Lycée Sihanouk in Kampong Cham (Lindsay French, personal communication 1989).

11. *Ĕthĭpol:* "greatness, power or influence (of authority), power of working wonders" (Headley, Jr., 1977:1452). This usage is quite unusual. While women are often discussed as being effective, as being able to accomplish things, they are rarely seen specifically as having power. See the discussion of Khmer terms for "power" as "male" in Ledgerwood (1990b:chap. 1). But Meung Tholla is *not* saying outright that women are "bigger" than men; in fact, a section at the end of the introduction emphasizes specifically that this is not the case. At times, when women might make such a case, the consequences are disastrous. See Meung Tholla (1981:12); see also the translation and discussion of this section in Ledgerwood (1990b:chap. 5).

12. On Khmer patron-client relationships in America, see Mortland and Ledgerwood (1987). On Khmer "female leadership" in the United States, see Shiori Ui (1991).

13. They will no doubt be distressed that I have highlighted the differences in the tellings. Each storyteller was most concerned to get the story right, that there was one correct way to tell a story. For a discussion of these concerns, see Ledgerwood (1990b:chap. 3).

14. I also argue elsewhere that for Khmer these gender conceptions are linked directly to notions of Khmer ethnicity (Ledgerwood 1990b).

10. Sharing the Pain

1. *Chaul vossa* is the beginning of the Buddhist period of retreat for monks for three months during the rainy season. This ceremony was observed

at the Site 2 center for displaced Khmer living on the Thailand border. Observations and interviews were also conducted at the Khao-I-Dang holding center during the last months of its operation.

2. A typical patient with Cushing's syndrome "has a rounded moon-shaped face, obesity with a 'buffalo hump' around the shoulders or a girdle distribution, a plethoric complexion associated with polycythemia, thin skin with easy bruising and abdominal striae, muscle weakness, hypertension, osteoporosis, and a diabetic type of glucose tolerance test" (Anderson 1971:1474).

11. Cultural Consumption

I thank Jackie Byars, Richard Lachmann, Ellen Rafferty, and two anonymous reviewers for their very helpful comments on earlier versions of this essay. I am also grateful to Carol Mortland for her editorial revisions of this chapter, which helped to focus and clarify many of my ideas. One of the earlier versions of this chapter was presented at the 1988 meeting of the Midwest Popular Culture Association at Bowling Green State University, Bowling Green, Ohio. My thanks also go to Pom Tam, Pom Tem, Van Chha Vun, and countless others for patient instruction in the Khmer language, and to Ses Chreb for first making me aware of the nature of peasant refugee perceptions of television.

1. The research represented here involved participant observation of Cambodian refugee television-viewing practices in Madison, Wisconsin, and Chicago, Illinois, over a two-year period. The most intensive observation was done during the summer of 1987 and involved an average of four hours of television viewing a day in the homes of approximately twelve Cambodian peasant refugees. This research was done in the context of a larger project concerning the description of Khmer peasant lifeways in the United States. This project included participation in many varieties of leisure activities, such as backyard gatherings and celebrations, in addition to television viewing. I also observed refugees' interactions with American institutions by translating for refugees in health-care and social-service settings. Finally, I was present during all manner of these peasants' economic production, including gardening, fishing, and everyday commercial transactions.

2. Dan Sperber (1982:179–80) goes so far as to label relativism (specifically, the view that traditional cultures may possess conceptions of reality which posit a supernatural world just as "real" to their members as the "rationalist" conception of reality supposedly widespread in the developed west) as a kind of "cognitive apartheid."

3. Perhaps the importance of viewing performance to Cambodians is indicated in the way that, in the literature (see Huffman and Proum 1972 and Pou 1983) as well as in the comments of Cambodian peasants, any given performance genre may be claimed at a given instance to be *the* favorite or *the*

most important to Cambodians. This pattern also shows the importance of individual variation in receiving "shared" cultural knowledge.

4. An important difference between the Cambodians' situation in the United States and their entertainment environment in prewar Cambodia or in the refugee camps is the frequency with which performance may be seen. In Cambodia, most performances occurred only in formal, festive contexts; see Pou (1983). In the west, drama and other forms of entertainment are available virtually on demand (see Williams 1975). It is no exaggeration to say that some form of drama, music, or dance performance—either traditional or western—may be viewed at literally any hour of the day or night, nonstop if desired.

5. Total commercial movie seating capacity in prewar Cambodia was estimated at 25,000 in 1974; radio receivers—a highly important means of villagers' exposure to the world outside Cambodia—were estimated to total 100,000. Television broadcasting began in Phnom Penh in 1966, but never covered much more than the immediate urban area (the total number of television sets in the country in 1971 was around 7,000). Broadcasting time probably never surpassed ten hours a week; see Lichty and Hoffer (1978).

6. John Marcucci, in his study of Cambodian refugees in Dallas (Marcucci 1986), notes that refugees often purchase VCRs and color TVs before they have attained financial stability. Conquergood (1986:1–3, 5) made similar observations among Lao refugees in Illinois.

7. The television set in American homes has been described as serving a similar central "family hearth" type role; see Adler (1975) and Ellis (1982).

8. For more on the tremendous impact of the Indian *Ramayana* classic in Cambodian and other Southeast Asian cultures, see Iyengar (1983).

9. One popular serial made in Hong Kong is taped in Boston from rented tapes by the relatives of a Cambodian family living in Wisconsin. Hours and hours of episodes of the program arrive every few months in the mail, and are watched virtually nonstop for days.

10. Often the dubbing in an entire film is done by just one or two males, who also read the voices of women and small children. The resulting strained falsettos sound quite humorous or fake to the American observer, but no "aesthetic dissonance" occurs for the peasant Khmer viewer who does not understand dubbing. Once, when I remarked that what was supposed to be the voice of a five-year-old girl in a Chinese film was actually that of a grown man, I was greeted by stares of bewilderment from all present.

11. There is no attempt to censor such displays of "immorality" and keep them from children. All family members watch the frequent naked bodies and sexual acts on American cable television with rapt attention. Older Cambodian women constantly comment on such displays, partly for my benefit: "Oh, my god! Look at that! Shit! Cambodians would never do that, you know?" or "Cambodians would never let such acts be filmed."

12. An interesting example of an almost "purposeful" entry into that belief space is the case of George Lucas. Lucas apparently created his *Star Wars*

plots and creatures on the model of traditional myths, discovered in the works of Joseph Campbell; see Woodward (1989). It is small wonder, then, that they should be accepted so readily by people with a culture so steeped in the very type of myth that Campbell studied.

13. Often, however, poor peasant Khmer refugees conceptually associate themselves with their poor Hispanic, black, and Asian neighbors. Cambodian peasant refugees are acutely aware of their position in the ethnic underclass framework of American society, and regularly make comments such as "Oh, there aren't any of us poor people—Khmers, Hmong, blacks, Hispanics—in that neighborhood. There are only nice American houses there" ("Oh, Phoum nĕung kmean yoeng nĕak krâ; khmae, moung, kmav, ispani te. Sŏt tae phtĕah amerĭkăng l'â l'â"). Peasant refugee self-devaluation based on skin color is not uncommon, either. See Smith (1989).

14. The peasant refugees' mode of consumption of television and other American cultural artifacts firmly places these Khmer, in mainstream Americans' eyes, in the same aesthetic camp with the working-class fans of professional wrestling and other forms of cultural "kitsch." It is no small coincidence that many of Cambodian peasant refugees' aesthetic preferences, from forms of entertainment to home furnishings, echo those preferences typically assigned to "low" or "popular" cultural strata of American society; see Laumann and House (1970), Gans (1974), and Halle (1991). It would be interesting to examine some of the perceptions of television of other ethnic "subcultures" in the United States—both groups of third world origin such as Mexican immigrants and also disenfranchised minorities of American origin such as poor blacks—with some of the same issues in mind which I present here. Such an approach already exists to an extent in the work of Bower (1985), who discusses the use of television by low social status blacks to become educated about the (white) world, and to "vicariously participate" in a society in which they have been denied participation.

15. Although Cambodians have played little importance historically in the American third world labor force, their contemporary participation in the unskilled, underpaid labor force of third world origin in this country, be it in the factories of Lowell, Massachusetts, in the cucumber fields of northern Wisconsin, or in the assembly plants of the Silicon Valley in California, is striking. See Sassen-Koob (1983); and Fernandez-Kelly and Garcia (1989).

References

Ablin, David A., and Marlowe Hood, eds. 1987. *The Cambodian Agony.* Armonk, N.Y.: M. E. Sharpe.

Abrahams, Roger D. 1972. "Proverbs and Proverbial Expressions." In R. M. Dorson, ed., *Folklore and Folklife: An Introduction,* pp. 117–27. Chicago: University of Chicago Press.

Adler, Richard. 1975. "Understanding Television: An Overview of the Literature of the Medium as a Social and Cultural Force." In D. Cater and R. Adler, eds., *Television as a Social Force: New Approaches to TV Criticism,* pp. 23–47. New York: Praeger.

Anderson, W. A. D., ed. 1971. *Pathology,* 6th ed. 2 vols. St. Louis, Mo: C. V. Mosby.

Ang Chouléan. 1980. "Le philtre sneh: De la femme humaine à la femme surnaturelle." *Seksa Khmer* 1, 2:155–202.

———. 1981. "Sahakum Khmae Neu Srok Barang Neng Preah Buddhasasana" [The Cambodian community in France and Buddhism]." *Culture khmère,* April–September:116–26. Paris: Cedoreck.

———. 1982. "Grossesse et accouchement au Cambodge: Aspects rituals." *Asie du Sud-Est et Monde insulindien* 13, 1–4:87–109.

———. 1986. *Les êtres surnaturels dans la religion populaire khmère.* Collection Bibliothèque khmère, Série Travaux et Recherches. Paris: Cedoreck.

———. 1988. "The Place of Animism within Popular Buddhism in Cambodia: The Example of the Monastery." *Asian Folklore Studies* 47, 1:35–41.

Anonymous. 1981. *Kap thmey dey Srăh Kaev* [New poems from Srah Keo]. Bangkok.

Ashe, Var Hong. 1988. *From Phnom Penh to Paradise.* London.

Bach, Robert L. 1986. "Immigration: Issues of Ethnicity, Class, and Public Policy in the United States." *Annals of the American Academy of Political and Social Science* 485:139–52.

Bateson, Gregory, and Mary Catherine Bateson. 1987. *Angels Fear: Towards an Epistemology of the Sacred.* New York: Macmillan.

Becker, Elizabeth. 1986. *When the War Was Over: The Voices of Cambodia's Revolution and Its People.* New York: Simon and Schuster.

Berry, Gordon L. 1980. "Television and Afro-Americans: Past Legacy and Present Portrayals." In S. B. Withey and R. P. Abeles eds., *Television and Social Behavior: Beyond Violence and Children,* pp. 231–48. Hillsdale, N.J.: Lawrence Erlbaum.

Bhargava, S. 1987. "Divine Sensation." *India Today,* April:170–71.

Biv Chhay Lieng. 1989. *Beh daung mae kântal sneh kâm* [Mother's heart in the midst of anguished love]. 2 vols. Paris.

Bizot, Française. 1976. *Le figuier a cinq branches—Recherche sur le Bouddhisme khmer.* Paris: École Française d'Extrême-Orient.

——. 1980. "Recherches sur le Bouhhdisme khmer. II. La grotte de la naissance." *Bulletin de l'École Française d'Extrême-Orient* 67:221–73.

——. 1981. "The Reamker." In I. K. R. Srinivasa ed., *Asian Variations in the Ramayana,* pp. 263–75. New Delhi: Sahitya Akademi.

Blumenthal, Eileen. 1989. "Picking up the Pieces of Cambodian Culture." *Asian Wall Street Journal,* January 27 and 28.

Boddy, William. 1983. "Loving a Nineteen-inch Motorola: American Writing on Television." In E. Ann Kaplan, ed., *Regarding Television: Critical Approaches—An Anthology,* pp. 1–11. Los Angeles: University Publications of America (American Film Institute).

Bogart, Leo. 1956. *The Age of Television.* London: Crosby Lockwood.

Boua, Chanthou. 1981. *Women in Kampuchea.* Bangkok: UNICEF.

——. 1982. Women in Today's Cambodia. *New Left Review* 131:45–61.

Bourdieu, Pierre. 1984. *Distinction: A Social Critique of the Judgement of Taste.* Trans. R. Nice. Cambridge, Mass.: Harvard University Press.

Bower, Robert T. 1985. *The Changing Television Audience in America.* New York: Columbia University Press.

Brandon, James R. 1967. *Theatre in Southeast Asia.* Cambridge, Mass.: Harvard University Press.

Brown, Mac H., et al. 1979. "Young Children's Perception of the Reality of Television." *Contemporary Education* 50, 3:129–33.

Buddhist Institute. 1971. *Bŏrâs kămchĭl mean brâpŭan krŭap lĕakkh* [The lazy man who had a perfect wife]. Phnom Penh: Buddhist Institute. (In *Brâchŭm reuang préng khmae* [Collection of Khmer folk tales] 1, 26, pp. 149–52.)

——. N.d. *Sâmlănh Pi Nĕak* [The two friends]. Phnom Penh: Buddhist Institute. (In *Brâchŭm reuang préng khmae* [Collection of Khmer folk tales] 1, 18, pp. 111–116.)

Cambodia, Ministry of Education. 1976. *Phoumĭsah Kâmpŭchea Brâcheathĭbbâtey* [Geography of Democratic Kampuchea]. Phnom Penh.

——. 1982a. *Kămrâng âtthâbât âksâ sĕl* [Collection of literary texts]. Phnom Penh: Fifth Level.

——. 1982b. *Kămrâng âtthâbât âksâ sěl* [Collection of literary texts]. Phnom Penh: Seventh Level.

——. 1984. *Kămrâng âtthâbât aksârsah* [Collection of literary texts]. Phnom Penh: Sixth Level.

——. 1986. *Cămrieng bâděvât* [Revolutionary songs]. Phnom Penh: Publications of the Cultural Foundation.

Cambodia, Ministry of Information. 1965. *La femme cambodgienne à l'ère du Sangkum*. Phenom Penh.

Carney, Timothy M., ed. 1977. *Communist Party Power in Kampuchea [Cambodia]: Documents and Discussion*. Ithaca: Cornell University, Southeast Asia Program. (Southeast Asia Program, Data Paper No. 106.)

Carpenter, Edmund. 1972. *Oh, What a Blow That Phantom Gave Me!* New York: Holt, Rinehart and Winston.

Catlin, Amy, ed. 1987. *Aspara: The Feminine in Cambodian Art*. Los Angeles: Woman's Building.

Chalmers, R. 1932. *Buddha's Teachings. Being the Sutta-Nipāta or Discourse Collection*. Cambridge, Mass.: Harvard University Press.

Chămrieng Bâděvât. N.d. Vol. 3. France: Comité des Patriotes du Kampuchea Démocratique en France.

Chanda, N. 1986. *Brother Enemy: The War after the War*. New York: Harcourt, Brace, Jovanovich.

Chandler, David P. 1974. "Cambodia before the French: Politics in a Tributary Kingdom." Ph.D. diss., Department of History, University of Michigan.

——. 1982. "Songs at the Edge of the Forest: Perceptions of Order in Three Cambodian Texts. In D. K. Wyatt and A. Woodside, eds., *Moral Order and the Question of Change: Essays on Southeast Asian Thought*, pp. 53–77. New Haven, Conn.: Yale University. (Southeast Asia Studies, Monograph Series No. 24.)

——. 1983. *A History of Cambodia*. Boulder, Colo.: Westview Press.

——. 1991. *The Tragedy of Cambodian History: Politics, War, and Revolution*. New Haven, Conn.: Yale University Press.

Chandler, David P., and Ben Kiernan, eds. 1983. *Revolution and Its Aftermath in Kampuchea: Eight Essays*. New Haven, Conn.: Yale University. (Southeast Asia Studies, Monograph Series No. 25.)

Chandler, David P., Ben Kiernan, and Chanthou Boua, eds. 1988. *Pol Pot Plans the Future. Confidential Leadership Documents from Democratic Kampuchea, 1976–1977*. New Haven, Conn.: Yale University. (Southeast Asia Studies, Monograph Series No. 33.)

Chapman, C. Richard. 1984. "New Directions in the Understanding and Management of Pain." *Social Science and Medicine* 19, 12:1261–77.

Chau Seng. 1962. *L'organisation buddhique au Cambodge*. Phnom Penh: Preah Sihanouk Raj Buddhist University.

Chbăp brŏs chbăp srey. *Chbăp brŏs chbăp srey* [Didactic codes for men and women]. Phnom Penh.

References

Cheriyand, K. C., and E. V. K. FitzGerald. 1989. *Development Planning in the State of Cambodia*. Phnom Penh: Non-Governmental Forum in Cambodia.

Chhai Si Nariddh and Kusal Phirum. 1986. *Vĭrochŭan Touch Phăn* [The hero, Toch Phann]. Phnom Penh: Publications of the Cultural Foundation.

Chheng Phon and Pech Tum Krâvel. 1986 *Dămnaoe cheat Kâmpŭchea* [The march forward of the Cambodian nation]. Phnom Penh: Publications of the Cultural Foundation.

Ching Sophon. 1982a. *Khleat srŏk kămnaoet* [Away from the homeland]. Bangkok.

——. 1982b. *Vĭmean moccŏreach* [The palace of death]. Bangkok.

Chuon Men. 1980. *Moel phaen ti Khmae sâmay Pŏl Pot—leng Sari* [A view of the map of Cambodia during the Pol Pot—leng Sary period]. Phnom Penh: Cambodia, Ministry of Information and Culture.

Coedès, Georges. 1956. "The Twenty-Five Hundredth Anniversary of the Buddha." *Diogenes* 15:95–111.

Coleman, Cynthia M. 1987. "Cambodians in the United States." In D. A. Ablin and M. Hood, eds., *The Cambodian Agony*, pp. 354–74. Armonk, N.Y.: M. E. Sharpe.

Collier, Jane F., and Sylvia J. Yanagisako. 1987. *Gender and Kinship: Essays towards a Unified Analysis*. Palo Alto, Calif.: Stanford University Press.

Conquergood, Dwight. 1986. "Is It real?"—Watching Television with Laotian Refugees." *Directions* 2, 2:1–3, 5.

Criddle, Joan and Mam Teeda Butt. 1987. *To Destroy You is No Loss: The Odyssey of a Cambodian Family*. New York: Atlantic Monthly Press.

Crystal, Eric. 1988. "Fragments of a Civilization." In R. A. Judkins, ed., *First International Scholars Conference on Cambodia, Selected Papers*, pp. 13–22. Geneseo, N.Y.: SUNY Department of Anthropology and the Geneseo Foundation.

Dao Noeu. 1987. [*Pyŭh chivĭt;* The violent storm of life]. Phnom Penh: Publications of the Cultural Foundation.

Delvert, Jean. 1961. *Le paysan cambodgien*. Paris: Mouton.

——. 1983. *Le Cambodge*. Paris: Presses universitaires de France.

DiMaggio, Paul. 1987. "Classification in Art." *American Sociological Review* 52, August:440–55.

Donnelly, Nancy D. 1989. "The Changing Lives of Refugee Hmong Women." Ph.D. diss. Department of Anthropology, University of Washington.

Dyphon, Pauline. 1988. "Suggestions for a Museum of Cambodian Ethnography in Washington D.C." In R. A. Judkins, ed., *First International Scholars Conference on Cambodia, Selected Papers*, pp. 5–7. Geneseo, N.Y.: SUNY Department of Anthropology and the Geneseo Foundation.

Eberhardt, Nancy. 1988. "Siren Song: Negotiating Gender Images in a Rural Shan Village." In N. Eberhardt, ed., *Gender, Power, and the Construction of the Moral Order: Studies from the Thai Periphery*, pp. 73–90. Madison, Wis.: University of Wisconsin-Madison. (Center for Southeast Asian Studies, Monograph Series No. 4.)

Ebihara, May M. 1966. "Interrelations between Buddhism and Social Systems in Cambodian Peasant Culture." In M. Nash et al., *Anthropological Studies in Theravada Buddhism*, pp. 175–96. New Haven, Conn.: Yale University. (Southeast Asia Studies, Cultural Report Series No. 13.)

———. 1968. "Svay, a Khmer Village in Cambodia." Ph.D. diss., Department of Anthropology, Columbia University.

———. 1974. "Khmer Village Women in Cambodia." In C. J. Matthiasson, ed., *Many Sisters: Women in Cross-cultural Perspective*, pp. 305–47. New York: Free Press.

———. 1985. "Khmer." In D. W. Haines, ed., *Refugees in the United States: A Reference Handbook*, pp. 127–47. Westport, Conn.: Greenwood Press.

———. 1987. "Revolution and Reformulation in Kampuchean Village Culture." In D. Ablin and M. Hood, eds., *The Cambodian Agony*, pp. 16–61. Armonk, N.Y.: M. E. Sharpe.

———. 1993. *"Beyond Suffering": The Recent History of a Cambodian Village.* In B. Ljunggren, ed. *The Challenge of Reform in Indochina*, pp. 149–66. Cambridge, Mass.: Harvard Institute for International Development and Harvard University Press. (Harvard Studies in International Development, vol. 2.)

Ellis, John. 1982. *Visible Fictions: Cinema, Television, Video.* London: Routledge and Kegan Paul.

Enzensberger, Hans M. 1986. "Constituents of a Theory of the Media." In J. G. Hanhardt, ed., *Video Culture: A Critical Investigation*, pp. 96–123. Rochester, N.Y.: Visual Studies Workshop Press.

Fawcett, B. 1988. *Cambodia: A Book for People Who Find Television Too Slow.* New York: Grove Press.

Fernandez-Kelly, M. Patricia, and Anna M. Garcia. 1989. "Information at the Core: Hispanic Women, Home Work and the Advanced Capitalist State." In A. Portes et al., eds., *The Informal Economy in Advanced and Less Developed Countries*, pp. 247–64. Baltimore, Md.: The John Hopkins University Press.

Finot, Louis. 1904. "Proverbes cambodgiens." *Revue indochinoise* 7:2.

Florentine Films. 1991. *Rebuilding the Temple.* [Film.]

Foucault, Michel. 1979. *Discipline and Punish: The Birth of the Prison.* Trans. A. Sheridan. New York: Pantheon.

Fouquet, David. 1981. "Buying American: Much of the World now Speaks with an American Accent and Punctuates Conversations with TV-Taught Yankee Slang." *Emmy* 3 (Fall):29.

French, Lindsay. 1990. "Marriage Patterns and Gender Relations in Site II, Thailand: Some Sociological Effects of a Peculiar Economy." Paper presented at the Annual Meetings, Association for Asian Studies, New Orleans.

Frieson, Kate. 1990. "The Pol Pot Legacy in Village Life." *Cultural Survival Quarterly* 14, 3:71–73.

———. 1992. "The Impact of the Revolution on Khmer Peasants: 1970–1975." Ph.D. diss., Department of Political Science, Monash University.

Frings, Viviane. 1993. *The Failure of Agricultural Collectivization in the People's Republic of Kampuchea (1979–1989)*. Clayton, Australia: Monash University, Centre of Southeast Asian Studies, Working Paper No. 80.

Gans, Herbert J. 1974. *Popular Culture and High Culture*. New York: Basic Books.

Gardner, Howard. 1985. "Cracking the Codes of Television: The Child as Anthropologist." In P. D. Agostino, ed., *Transmission*, pp. 93–102. New York: Tanam Press.

Geertz, Clifford. 1966. "Religion as a Cultural System." In M. Banton, ed., *Anthropological Approaches to the Study of Religion*, pp. 1–46. London: Tavistock (A.S.A. [Association of Social Anthropologists of the Commonwealth] Monograph 3.)

———. 1968. *Islam Observed: Religious Development in Morocco and Indonesia*. New Haven, Conn.: Yale University Press.

———. 1973. *The Interpretation of Cultures*. New York: Basic Books.

Gihivinaya Samkhepa. 1963. [Pali texts with Khmer translation] by Brah Guru Vimalapanna Oum-Sou and Brah Guru Samsattha Chuon-Nath. 21st ed. Phnom Penh: Buddhist Institute.

Gombrich, Richard, and Gananath Obeyesekere. 1988. *Buddhism Transformed: Religious Change in Sri Lanka*. Princeton, N.J.: Princeton University Press.

Gonzalez, Nancy L., and C. S. McCommon. 1989. *Conflict, Migration, and the Expression of Ethnicity*. Boulder, Colo.: Westview Press.

Good, B., and M. D. Good. 1981. "The Meaning of Symptoms: A Cultural Hermeneutic Model for Clinical Practice." In L. Eisenberg and A. Kleinman, eds., *The Relevance of Social Science for Medicine*, pp. 165–96. Dordrecht, The Netherlands: D. Reidel.

Gramsci, Antonio. 1957. *The Modern Prince and Other Writings*. Trans. L. Marks. New York: International Publishers.

Greenberg, B. S., and Byron Reeves. 1976. "Children and the Perceived Reality of Television." *Journal of Social Issues* 32, 4:86–97.

Haines, David W., ed. 1985. *Refugees in the United States: A Reference Handbook*. Westport, Conn.: Greenwood Press.

Hall, Stuart. 1980. "Encoding/Decoding." In S. Hall et al., eds., *Culture, Media, Language: Working Papers in Cultural Studies, 1972–1979*, pp. 128–38. London: Hutchinson.

Halle, D. 1991. "Bringing Materialism Back In: Art in the Houses of the Working and Middle Classes in Bringing Class Back." In S. G. McNall, R. F. Levine and R. Fantasia, eds., *Contemporary and Historical Perspectives*, pp. 241–59. Boulder, Colo.: Westview Press.

Hanks, Lucien M., and Jane Hanks. 1963. "Thailand: Equality between the Sexes." In B. Ward, ed., *Women in the New Asia*, pp. 424–51. Amsterdam: UNESCO.

Hansen, Anne R. 1988. "Crossing the River: The Secularization of the Khmer Religious Worldview." M.A. thesis, Harvard University.

Hansen, Anne R., and Bounthay Phath. 1987. "Understanding Suffering in the Context of Khmer Buddhism: Preliminary Research Observations." Unpublished paper, Harvard University.

Headley, Robert, Jr. 1977. *Cambodian-English Dictionary.* Washington D.C.: Catholic University of America Press.

Heder, Stephen R. 1980a. *Kampuchean Occupation and Resistance.* Bangkok: Chulalongkorn University Institute of Asian Studies. (Asian Studies Monograph No. 27.)

———. 1980b. "Stephen Heder on Cambodia 1979." Unpublished monograph, U.S. Department of State.

———. 1980c. "Thirty-eight Interviews in February–March." Unpublished typescript.

———. 1981. "Kampuchea 1980: Anatomy of a Crisis." *Southeast Asia Chronicle* 77:3–11.

Hefner, Robert W. 1985. *Hindu Javanese: Tengger Tradition and Islam.* Princeton, N.J.: Princeton University Press.

Hickey, Gerald C. 1982. *Free in the Forest: Ethnohistory of the Vietnamese Central Highlands, 1954–1976.* New Haven, Conn.: Yale University Press.

Hobsbawn, Eric, and Terence Ranger. 1983. *The Invention of Tradition.* New York: Cambridge University Press.

Hodge, James L. 1988. "New-Bottles-Old-Wine: The Persistence of the Heroic Figure in the Mythology of Television in Science-Fiction." *Journal of Popular Culture* 21, 4:37–48.

Hodge, Robert, and David Tripp. 1986. *Children and Television: A Semiotic Approach.* Stanford, Calif.: Stanford University Press.

Hoe Sokhai. 1984. *Thngai lĭc nôv phoum Phâl* [The sun sets at Phal village]. Phnom Penh: Publications of the Cultural Foundation.

Huffman, Franklin E. 1972. *Intermediate Cambodian Reader.* New Haven, Conn.: Yale University Press.

Huffman, Franklin E., and Im Proum. 1977. *Cambodian Literary Reader and Glossary.* New Haven, Conn.: Yale University Press.

Ieng Mouly. 1986. "Causes of the Suffering and the Options of a Strategy to Rebuild the Khmer Society." In *Buddhism and the Future of Cambodia*, pp. 28–69. Rithisen, Thailand: Khmer Buddhist Research Center.

Ing Kien. 1977. [*Phka chhouk Kâmpŭchea*; Lotus flower of Cambodia]. Paris: Anakota.

International Rescue Committee. 1985. *Sŏk Sâbay.* August, September, December issues. Khao I Dang, Thailand: Education Development Center.

Ishii, Yoneo. 1976. "A note on Buddhist Millenarian Revolts in Northeastern Siam." In S. Ichimura, ed., *Southeast Asia: Nature, Society and Development*, pp. 67–75. Honolulu: University Press of Hawaii.

Ith Sarin. 1977. "Nine Months with the Marquis and Life in the Bureaus (offices) of Phnom Penh." In T. Carney, ed., *Communist Party Power in Kampuchea (Cambodia): Documents and Discussion*, pp. 34–55. Ithaca: Cornell University. (Southeast Asia Program, Data Paper No. 106.)

Iv Huot. N.d. *Veasâna ângko* [The destiny of Angkor]. Paris.

Iyengar, K. R. Srivivasa, ed. 1983. *Asian Variations in Ramayana.* Madras: Sahitya Akademi.

Jackson, Karl D., ed. 1989. *Cambodia, 1975–1978: Rendezvous with Death.* Princeton, N.J.: Princeton University Press.

Jones, Clayton. 1987. "Cambodians Revive Classical Dance after Near-Destruction of Heritage." *Christian Science Monitor,* June 17.

Kalab, Milada. 1968. "Study of a Cambodian Village." *Geographical Journal,* 134, 4:521–34.

———. 1990. "Buddhism and Emotional Support for Elderly People." *Journal of Cross-Cultural Gerontology,* 7–19.

Kampuchea Review. 1979. "Phnom Penh Reports Membership of New KNUFNS Central Committee." 4, October 30, p. H1.

———. 1982. "Chheng Phon [and] Others Address Drama Day Ceremony." 4, March 31, p. H1.

Kampuchea Today. 1988. Phnom Penh: Cambodia, Ministry of Information and Culture.

Kapferer, Bruce. 1988. *Legends of People, Myths of State: Violence, Intolerance, and Political Culture in Sri Lanka and Australia.* Washington, D.C.: Smithsonian Institution Press.

Kaplan, David A. 1989. "Film about a Fatal Beating Examines a Community." *New York Times,* July 17:27, 32.

Katz, Elihu, and Tamar Liebes. 1987. "Decoding 'Dallas': Notes from a Cross-cultural Study." In H. Newcomb, ed., *Television: The Critical View,* 4th ed., pp. 419–32. New York: Oxford University Press.

Kaye, Jeff. 1987. "News Update: Chinese Choose [Welby], [Star Trek], Two Others." *TV Guide* 35, February 15:44. [Words in brackets were in Chinese.]

Kchao Vaddhana. 1989. "Khmer: The Lost Generation." *Changing East Asia* 9, 1:12–13.

Kèo Chanda. 1983. *Sŏphĕak mongkŭal knŏng kruosa kâsĕkâ* [The happiness of a peasant family]. Phnom Penh. [newspaper].

Keyes, Charles F. 1977. *The Golden Peninsula: Culture and Adaptation in Mainland Southeast Asia.* New York: Macmillan.

———. 1984. "Mother or Mistress but Never a Monk: Buddhist Notions of Female Gender in Rural Thailand." *American Ethnologist* 11, 2:223–41.

Keyes, Charles F., and E. Valentine Daniel, eds. 1983. *Karma: An Anthropological Inquiry.* Berkeley: University of California Press.

Khiev Kanharith, Chiva, and Khim Sarâng. *Péch Pailĭn—Choup knea kraoy phlieng thlĕak—Nhonhĕum cŏng kraoy* [The diamond of Pailin—Meet after the rain has fallen—The last smile]. Phnom Penh: [newspaper].

Khing Hoc Dy. 1977. "Notes sur le thème de la femme 'marquée des signes' dans la littérature populaire khmère." *Cahiers de l'Asie du Sud-Est* 2:15–43.

———. 1980. "Quelques aspects de la beauté de la femme dans la littérature populaire khmère." *Seksa Khmer* 1–2:45–68.

——. 1989. "Contribution à l'histoire de la littérature khmère." *L'Époque classique (XVe–XIXe siècles)*. Vol. 1. Paris: L'Harmattan.

——. 1992. "Contribution à l'histoire de la littérature khmère." *L'Époque moderne et contemporaine (1900–1990)*. Vol. 2. Paris: L'Harmattan.

Kiernan, Ben. 1985. *How Pol Pot Came to Power*. London: Verso.

——. 1988. "Planning the Past: The Forced Confessions of Hu Nim" [Tuol Sleng Prison, May–June 1977, 105 pp., handwritten]. In D. P. Chandler, B. Kiernan, and C. Boua, eds., *Pol Pot Plans the Future: Confidential Leadership Documents from Democratic Kampuchea, 1976–1977*, pp. 227–317. New Haven, Conn.: Yale University. (Southeast Asia Studies, Monograph Series No. 33.)

——. 1989. "The American Bombardment of Kampuchea, 1969–1973." *Vietnam Generation* 1, 1:3–39.

——. 1990. "The Genocide in Cambodia, 1975–1979." *Bulletin of Concerned Asian Scholars* 22, 3:35–40.

Kiernan, Ben, and Chanthou Boua, eds. 1982. *Peasants and Politics in Kampuchea, 1942–1981*. London: Zed Books.

Kil Samdol. N.d. *Nokor něak léng* [Kingdom of the thugs]. Bangkok.

Kim Pech Pinonn. 1984. *Pou Kŭn, kâsěkâr* [Uncle Kun, the peasant]. Phnom Penh: Publications of the Cultural Foundation.

——. 1986. *Těuk chět bâng* [My heart]. Phnom Penh: Publications of the Cultural Foundation.

Kim Phann Tara. 1981. *Sâng sǒek* [Vengeance]. Bangkok.

Kinzie, J. D. 1987. "The 'Concentration Camp' Syndrome." In D. A. Ablin and M. Hood, eds., *The Cambodian Agony*, pp. 332–53. Armonk, N.Y.: M. E. Sharpe.

Kirsch, A. Thomas. 1981. "The Thai Buddhist Quest for Merit." In *Clues to Thai Culture*, pp. 120–36. Bangkok: Central Thai Language Committee.

——. 1982. "Buddhism, Sex-roles and the Thai Economy." In P. Van Esterik, ed., *Women in Southeast Asia*, pp. 16–41. DeKalb, Ill.: Northern Illinois University. (Center for Southeast Asian Studies, Occasional Paper 7.)

——. 1984. "Text and Context: Buddhist Sex Roles/Culture of Gender Revisited." *American Ethnologist* 12, 2:302–20.

Kong Boun Chhoeun. 1980. *Ântat phloeng knŏng duong prolěung* [Flames of fire in the spirit]. Phnom Penh.

——. 1987a. *Něak daoe kǎt pyüh* [Those who cross the violent storm]. Phnom Penh: Publications of the Cultural Foundation.

——. 1987b. *Slǒek chhoe chak Mêk* [The leaves fall from the trees]. Phnom Penh: Publications of the Cultural Foundation.

Lakoff, George, and Mark Johnson. 1980. *Metaphors We Live By*. Chicago: University of Chicago Press.

Lapsley, Robert, and Michael Westlake. 1988. *Film Theory: An Introduction*. Manchester: Manchester University Press.

Laumann, Edward O., and J. S. House. 1970. "Living Room Styles and Social Attributes: The Patterning of Material Artifacts in a Modern Urban Community." *Sociology and Social Research* 54:321–42.

LaValley, Albert J. 1985. "Traditions of Trickery: The Role of Special Effects in the Science Fiction Film." In G. Slusser and E. S. Rabkin, eds., *Shadows of the Magic Lamp: Fantasy and Science Fiction in Film*, pp. 141–58. Carbondale: Southern Illinois University Press.

Leach, Edmund R. 1968. *Dialectic in Practical Religion*. Cambridge: Cambridge University Press.

Ledgerwood, Judy. 1989. KG-JL-A [tapes]. Washington, D.C.: Library of Congress, Indochina Archive.

——. 1990a. "A Building Full of Books." *Cultural Survival Quarterly*, 14, 3:53–55.

——. 1990b. "Changing Khmer Conceptions of Gender: Women, Stories, and the Social Order." Ph.D. diss., Departments of Anthropology and the Southeast Asia Program, Cornell University.

——. 1990c. "Portrait of a Conflict: Exploring Khmer—American Social and Political Relationships." *Journal of Refugee Studies* 3, 2:135–54.

——. 1992. *Analysis of the Situation of Women in Cambodia*. Phnom Penh: UNICEF.

Levine, Robert A. 1984. "Properties of Culture: An Ethnographic View." In R. Shweder and R. Levine, eds., *Culture Theory: Essays on Mind, Self and Emotion*, pp. 67–87. Cambridge: Cambridge University Press.

Lichty, Lawrence W., and Thomas W. Hoffer. 1978. "North Vietnam, Khmer, and Laos." In J. A. Lent, ed., *Broadcasting in Asia and the Pacific: A Continental Survey of Radio and Television*, pp. 111–22. Philadelphia: Temple University Press.

Lipton, James A., and Joseph J. Marbach. 1984. "Ethnicity and the Pain Experience." *Social Science and Medicine* 19, 12:1279–98.

Lon Van. 1981. *Tâsou knŏng bâthâmâvay* [The struggle in the first age]. Bangkok.

MacCormack, Carol P., and Marilyn Strathern. 1980. *Nature, Culture and Gender*. Cambridge: Cambridge University Press.

McGinnis, Joe. 1981. "Welcome to Alaska, 'Six million dollar man': Watching Television Is Now as Vital to Alaskan Villages as Skinning Foxes and Weaving Traps." *Panorama* 2, April:38.

Maranda, Elli K. 1978. "Folklore and Culture Change: Lau Riddles of Modernization." In R. M. Dorson, ed., *Folklore in the Modern World*, pp. 207–18. The Hague: Mouton.

March, Kathryn S. 1983. "Weaving, Writing and Gender." *Man* 18:729–44.

Marcucci, John. 1986. "Khmer Refugees in Dallas: Medical Decisions in the Context of Pluralism." Ph.D. diss., Department of Anthropology, Southern Methodist University.

Marcus, George E. 1989. "The Problem of the Unseen World of Wealth for the Rich: Toward an Ethnography of Complex Connections." *Ethos* 17, 1:114–23.

Marston, John, with Sotheary Duong. 1988. "Language Use and Language Policy in Democratic Kampuchea." Paper presented at an Indochina Studies

Program Colloquium on Language Use and Language Policy in Laos, Cambodia, and Vietnam. University of Hawaii, June 27–28.

Martin, Marie A. 1986. "Vietnamised Cambodia: A Silent Ethnocide." *Indochina Report* 7:1–31.

May Someth. 1986. *Cambodian Witness: The Autobiography of Someth May.* London: Faber and Faber.

Meung Tholla. 1981. *Vĭcchea ắp rŭm strey khmae* [The science of raising girl children]. Khao-I-Dang, Thailand: International Rescue Committee.

Migozzi, J. 1973. *Cambodge: Faits et problèmes de population.* Paris: Centre national de la Recherche scientifique.

Mills, M. L. 1968. "Health Education in a Cambodian Village." *U.S. Public Health Reports* 83:898.

Mollica, Richard F. 1987. "The Trauma Story: The Psychiatric Case of Refugee Survivors of Violence and Torture." In F. M. Ochberg, ed., *Post-Traumatic Therapy and the Victim of Violence.* New York: Brunner-Mazel.

Moore, Sally Falk. 1986. *Social Facts and Fabrications: "Customary Law" on Kilimanjaro, 1880–1980.* Cambridge: Cambridge University Press.

Mortland, Carol A. 1987. "Transforming Refugees in Refugee Camps." *Urban Anthropology* 16, 3–4:375–404.

Mortland, Carol A., and Judy Ledgerwood. 1987. "Refugee Resource Acquisition: The Invisible Communication System." In Y. Y. Kim and W. B. Gudykunst, eds., *Cross-Cultural Adaptation: Current Approaches,* pp. 286–306. Newbury Park, Calif.: Sage.

Muecke, Marjorie. 1981. "Changes in Women's Status Associated with Modernization in Northern Thailand." In G. B. Hainsworth, ed., *Southeast Asia: Women, Changing Social Structure and Cultural Continuity,* pp. 53–65. Ottawa: University of Ottawa Press.

Myerhoff, Barbara. 1978. *Number Our Days.* New York: Simon and Schuster.

Mysliwiec, Eva. 1988. *Punishing the Poor: The International Isolation of Kampuchea.* Oxford: Oxfam.

Newcomb, Horace, ed. 1987. *Television: The Critical View.* 4th ed. New York: Oxford University Press.

Ngor Haing. 1987. *A Cambodian Odyssey.* New York: Macmillan.

Ngy Chanphal. 1987. Correspondence from Khmer Studies Institute, July. Newington, Conn.

Nong Thierry. 1982. *Knŏng muoy chivĭt* [In one life]. Bangkok.

——. N.d. *Neh haoey pie* [This is the fruit of your bad deeds]. Bangkok.

Nonn Chan. 1983. *Phka rik pél ârŭn rĕah* [The flower blossoms at dawn]. Phnom Penh: Publications of the Cultural Foundation.

——. 1986. *Phlieng rodauv ktav* [Rain in the hot season]. Phnom Penh: Publications of the Cultural Foundation.

——. 1988a. *Câmrieng chivĭt* [Songs of life]. Phnom Penh: Publications of the Cultural Foundation.

———. 1988b. *Praleŭng Kesâ Kŏl* [The soul of Kesar Kol]. Phnom Penh: Publications of the Cultural Foundation.

Nowak, Margie. 1984. *Tibetan Refugees.* New Brunswick, N.J.: Rutgers University Press.

Ortner, Sherry B. 1973. "On Key Symbols." *American Anthropologist* 75:1338–46.

———. 1974. "Is Female to Male as Nature Is to Culture?" In M. Z. Rosaldo and L. Lamphere, eds., *Women, Culture and Society,* pp. 67–88. Palo Alto, Calif.: Stanford University Press.

———. 1984. "Theory in Anthropology since the Sixties." *Comparative Studies in Society and History* 26, 1:126–66.

Ortner, Sherry, and Harriet Whitehead, eds. 1981. *Sexual Meanings: The Cultural Construction of Gender and Sexuality.* Cambridge: Cambridge University Press.

Pack, Susan. 1989. "Cambodian Odyssey." Long Beach, Calif., *Press-Telegram,* April 30, J1–J5.

Pal Vannariraks. 1988a. *Choeng mékh thmey nei ktey sângkhĕum* [The new horizon of hope]. Phnom Penh: Imprimerie de la capitale.

———. 1988b. *Ronôch phŏt haoey* [The waning moon has already passed]. Phnom Penh: Imprimerie de la capitale.

Pannetier, A. 1915. "Sentences et proverbes cambodgiens." *Bulletin de l'École Française d'Extrême-Orient* 15, 3:47–71.

Pech Tum Krâvel. 1983. *Măk Thoeung* [Mak Thoeng]. Phnom Penh: Cambodia, Ministry of Information and Culture.

Pèn Vann Thôn. 1983. *Yoeng btechnha lâh băng âvey âvey tĕang ăh daoembey sângkrŭah cheat nĭng meatŏphoum* [We resolutely decide to make every sacrifice to save the nation and the motherland]. Phnom Penh: Cambodia, Ministry of Information and Culture.

———. 1987. *Ânŭssavâri nei hemân rodauv* [Remembrances of winter]. Phnom Penh: Publications of the Cultural Foundation.

———. 1988a. *Chan rĕah chlâng daen* [The moonlight across the frontier]. Phnom Penh: Publications of the Cultural Foundation.

———. 1988b. *Reuang k'aek nĭng trey* [The story of the crow and the fish]. Phnom Penh: Publications of the Cultural Foundation.

Pok Ponn Sa Mach. 1988. *Yŭap kântal thngai* [Darkness in broad daylight]. Phnom Penh: Publications of the Cultural Foundation [newspaper].

Pol Saroeung. 1988. *Chĕt phĕaktey* [The faithful heart]. Phnom Penh: Publications of the Cultural Foundation [newspaper].

Ponchaud, Français. 1978. *Cambodia Year Zero.* London: Allen Lane.

———. 1989. "Social Change in the Vortex of Revolution." In K. D. Jackson, ed., *Cambodia 1975–1978: Rendezvous with Death,* pp. 151–77. Princeton, N.J.: Princeton University Press.

Porée-Maspero, Eveline. 1962–69. *Étude sur les rites agraires des Cambodgiens.* 3 vols. Paris: Mouton.

Potter, W. James. 1986. "Perceived Reality and the Cultivation Hypothesis." *Journal of Broadcasting and Electronic Media* 30, 2:159–74.

Pou, Saveros. 1983. "Ramakertian Studies." In S. Iyengar, ed., *Asian Variations in Ramayana*, pp. 252–62. Madras: Sahitya Akademi.

Reynell, J. 1989. *Political Pawns: Refugees on the Thai-Kampuchean Border.* Oxford: University of Oxford Refugee Studies Programme.

Robinson, Richard H., and Willard L. Johnson. 1982. *The Buddhist Religion: A Historical Introduction.* 3d ed. Belmont, Calif.: Wadsworth.

Rosaldo, Michelle Z. 1974. "Women, Culture and Society: A Theoretical Overview." In M. Z. Rosaldo and L. Lamphere, eds., *Women, Culture and Society*, pp. 17–42. Palo Alto, Calif.: Stanford University Press.

Ros Viriya. 1979. *Kraoy pél phlieng* [After the rain]. Paris: Angkor.

Sahlins, Marshall. 1982. "Individual Experience and Cultural Order." In W. Kruskal, ed., *The Social Sciences: Their Nature and Uses*, pp. 35–48. Chicago: University of Chicago Press.

———. 1985. *Islands of History.* Chicago: University of Chicago Press.

Sam-Ang Sam. 1987. *Traditional Music of Cambodia.* Middletown, Conn.: Center for the Study of Khmer Culture.

———. 1988. "The Pin Peat Ensemble: Its History, Music, and Context." Ph.D. diss., Department of Music, Wesleyan University.

Sam Sophâl. 1986a. *Rodauv phka rik* [Springtime]. Phnom Penh: Publications of the Cultural Foundation.

———. 1986b. *Snam dǎmbav* [The scar]. Phnom Penh: Publications of the Cultural Foundation.

———. 1987. *Sât reatrey châ* [Nocturnal animals]. Phnom Penh: Publications of the Cultural Foundation.

———. 1988. *Chǎmnâng sneh yǔveǎvay* [The ties of young love]. Phnom Penh: Publications of the Cultural Foundation.

Santoli, Al. 1988. "Voices from the Refugee Camps." In R. A. Judkins, ed., *First International Scholars Conference on Cambodia, Selected Papers*, pp. 9–12. Geneseo, N.Y.: SUNY Department of Anthropology and the Geneseo Foundation.

Sargent, Carolyn. 1984. "Between Death and Shame: Dimensions of Pain in Bariba Culture." *Social Science and Medicine* 19, 12:1299–1304.

Sargent, Carolyn, and John Macucci. 1984. "Aspects of Khmer Medicine among Refugees in Urban America." *Medical Anthropology Quarterly* 16, 1:7–9.

———. 1988. "Khmer Prenatal Health Practices and the American Clinical Experience." In Karen Michaelson, ed., *Childbirth in America*, pp. 79–89. Mass.: Bergin and Garvey.

Sargent, C., J. Macucci, and Ellen Elliston. 1983. "Tiger Bones, Fire and Wine: Maternity Care in a Kampuchean Refugee Community." *Medical Anthropology* 7, 4:67–79.

Sar Kapun. 1982. *Kǎmrâng kǎmnap* [Collection of poems]. Phnom Penh: Cambodia, Ministry of Information and Culture.

Sar Kapun and Yok Lun. 1985. *Tĕuk chĕt kâvi* [The poet's heart]. Phnom Penh: Publications of the Cultural Foundation.

Sâr Sieng Hieng. 1987. *Krŏap kămphloeng cŏng kraoy* [The last cartridge]. Phnom Penh: Publications of the Cultural Foundation.

Sassen-Koob, Saskia. 1983. "Labor Migrations and the New International Division of Labor." In J. Nash and M. P. Fernandez-Kelly, eds., *Women, Men, and the International Division of Labor*, pp. 175–204. Albany: State University of New York Press.

Sattaparitta-Dvadasaparitta. 1965. [Pali text with Khmer translation by] Préas Visuddhivong H. Tath. 6th [or 16th] ed. [French title page says 6th, Khmer title page says 16th.] Phnom Penh: Buddhist Institute.

Schanberg, Sidney H. 1972. "Cambodians Still Rely on Buddhism's Timeless Signs." *New York Times*, December 15.

Schieffelin, Edward L. 1979. "Mediators as Metaphors: Moving a Man to Tears in Papua, New Guinea." In A. L. Becker and A. A. Yengoyan, eds., *The Imagination of Reality: Essays in Southeast Asian Coherence Systems*, pp. 127–44. Norwood, N.J.: ABLEX.

———. 1985. "Performance and the Cultural Construction of Reality." *American Ethnologist* 12, 4:707–724.

Sem Sara. 1967. "Lokhon Khol au village de Vat Svay Andet, son rôle dans les rites agraires." *Annales de l'Université des Beaux Arts* 1:157–200.

Shawcross, William. 1979. *Sideshow: Kissinger, Nixon and the Destruction of Cambodia*. London: André Deutsch.

Sheehy, Gail. 1986. *Spirit of Survival*. New York: Morrow.

Siv, Darina. N.d. Personal memoirs.

Smith, Frank. 1989. *Interpretative Accounts of the Khmer Rouge Years: Personal Experience in Cambodian Peasant World View*. Madison, Wisc.: Center for Southeast Asian Studies, University of Wisconsin-Madison. (Wisconsin Papers on Southeast Asia, Occasional Paper No. 18.)

Sonnois, Brigitte. 1990. *Women in Cambodia*. Phnom Penh. Redd Barna.

Son Sann. 1986. "Buddhism and the Future of Cambodia." In *Buddhism and the Future of Cambodia*, pp. 157–63. Rithisen: Khmer Buddhist Research Center.

Soth Polin. 1980. "Pol Pot's Diabolical Sweetness." *Index on Censorship*, October: 34–45.

Sperber, Dan. 1982. "Apparently Irrational Beliefs." In M. Hollis and S. Lukes, eds., *Rationality and Relativism*, pp. 149–80. Cambridge, Mass.: M.I.T. Press.

Spiro, Melford. 1967. *Burmese Supernaturalism: A Study in the Explanation and Reduction of Suffering*. Englewood Cliffs, N.J.: Prentice-Hall.

———. 1970. *Buddhism and Society*. New York: Harper and Row.

Steinberg, David J., et al. 1959. *Cambodia: Its People, Its Society, Its Culture*. New Haven, Conn.: Human Relations Area Files Press.

Strathern, Marilyn. 1987. *Dealing with Inequality: Analyzing Gender Relations in Melanesia and Beyond*. Cambridge: Cambridge University Press.

Swain, J. 1985. "Return to the Killing Fields." *Sunday Times* (London), May 26.

Szymusiak, Molyda. 1986. *The Stones Cry Out.* Trans. L. Coverdale. New York: Hill and Wang.

Taing Veng. 1981. *Pa khŏs haoey kaun* [Your father is wrong, child]. Bangkok.

Tambiah, Stanley J. 1970. *Buddhism and the Spirit Cults in North-east Thailand.* Cambridge: Cambridge University Press.

——. 1976. *World Conqueror and World Renouncer.* Cambridge, Mass.: Cambridge University Press.

Tan Yim Phong. 1984. "Restaurants et ateliers: Le travail des sino-khmères à Paris. Cambodge II." *Asie du Sud-Est et Monde Insulindien* 15, 1–4: 277–91.

Tau Hing, ed. 1955. *Pheasĭt sâmray* [Proverbs]. Phnom Penh: Khemara Bannagar.

Thierry, Solange. 1958. "Essai sur les proverbes cambodgiens." *Revue de Psychologie des Peuples.* 13:431–43.

——. 1964. *Les Khmers.* Bourges: L'Imprimerie Tardy.

——. 1978. *Étude d'un corpus de contes cambodgiens traditionnels: Essai d'analyse thématique et morphologique.* Paris: Diffusion Librairie Honoré Champion.

——. 1985. *Le Cambodge des contes.* Paris: L'Harmattan.

Thion, S. 1983. "The Cambodian Idea of Revolution." In D. Chandler and B. Kiernan, eds., *Revolution and Its Aftermath in Kampuchea: Eight Essays,* pp. 10–33. New Haven, Conn.: Yale University Southeast Asia Studies. (Southeast Asia Studies, Monograph Series No. 25.)

Ti Chi Huot. 1984. *Vĭl rok tronŭm* [Return to our home]. Phnom Penh: Publications of the Cultural Foundation.

——. 1988. *Mékh băt duong chan* [A moonless sky]. Phnom Penh: Publications of the Cultural Foundation.

Tossânavâddey Roupheap. *Tossânavâddey Roupheap* [an illustrated journal]. 1976. December: 10–11. Phnom Penh.

Tŭang Bâdĕvât. 1976. Number 6.

Turner, Victor. 1967. *The Forest of Symbols.* Ithaca: Cornell University Press.

Twining, Charles H. 1989. "The Economy." In K. D. Jackson, ed., *Cambodia, 1975–1978: Rendezvous with Death,* pp. 109–50. Princeton, N.J.: Princeton University Press.

Ui, Shiori. 1991. " 'Unlikely heroes': The Evolution of Female Leadership in a Cambodian Ethnic Enclave." In M. Buraway et al., eds., *Ethnography Unbound: Power and Resistance in the Modern Metropolis,* pp. 161–77. Berkeley: University of California Press.

United Nations Children's Fund [UNICEF], Office of the Special Representative. 1990. *Cambodia: The Situation of Children and Women.* Phnom Penh.

United Nations High Commissioner for Refugees (UNHCR). 1980. *Rien âksâ Khmae thnăk 1* [Beginning Khmer reader 1]. Khao I Dang, Thailand: Education Development Center.

——. 1981a. *Rien âksâ Khmae thnăk 2* [Beginning Khmer reader 2]. Khao I Dang, Thailand: Education Development Center.

——. 1981b. *Rien âksâ Khmae thnăk 3* [Beginning Khmer reader 3]. Khao I Dang, Thailand: Education Development Center.

——. 1981c. *Rien âksâ Khmae thnăk 4* [Beginning Khmer reader 4]. Khao I Dang, Thailand: Education Development Center.

United States Committee for Refugees. 1990. *World Refugee Survey: 1989 in Review.* Washington, D.C.: American Council for Nationalities Service.

U.S. Bureau for Refugee Programs. 1990. *World Refugee Report, September 1990: A Report Submitted to the Congress as Part of the Consultation on FY1991 Refugee Admissions to the United States.* Washington, D.C.: Department of State Publication. (Department of State Publication 9802.).

Vandy Kaon. 1981. *Une réflexion sur la littérature khmère.* Phnom Penh: Institute of Sociology.

——. 1987a. *Kaoh beysach* [The island of evil spirits]. Phnom Penh: Institute of Sociology.

——. 1987b. *Reuang préng* [Folk tales]. Phnom Penh: Cambodia, Ministry of Education.

Van Esterik, Penny. 1980. "Cultural Factors Affecting the Adjustment of Southeast Asian Refugees." In E. Tepper, ed., *Southeast Exodus: From Tradition to Resettlement,* pp. 151–71. Ottawa: Canadian Asian Studies Association.

——. 1982. "Lay Women in Theravada Buddhism." In P. Van Esterik, ed., *Women in Southeast Asia,* pp. 55–78. DeKalb, Ill.: Northern Illinois University (Center for Southeast Asian Studies, Occasional Paper 9.)

Vann Chantha. 1984. *Kŏma khmav dai tĭp* [The children with a magical pencil]. Phnom Penh: Publications of the Cultural Foundation.

Veyne, Paul. 1988. *Did the Greeks Believe in Their Myths? An Essay on the Constitutive Imagination.* Trans. P. Wissing. Chicago, Ill.: University of Chicago Press.

Vickery, Michael. 1984. *Cambodia, 1975–1982.* Boston, Mass.: South End Press.

——. 1986. *Kampuchea: Politics, Economics, and Society.* Boulder, Colo.: Lynne Riener.

——. 1987. "Refugee Politics: The Khmer Camps System in Thailand." In D. A. Ablin and M. Hood, eds., *The Cambodian Agony,* pp. 293–331. Armonk, N.Y.: M. E. Sharpe.

Volkman, Toby, ed. 1990. "Cambodia, 1990." *Cultural Survival Quarterly* 14, 3.

Weisenberg, M., ed. 1975. *Pain: Clinical and Experimental Perspectives.* St. Louis, Mo.: C. V. Mosby

Williams, Raymond. 1975. *Television: Technology and Cultural Form.* New York: Schocken Books.

Willmott, William E. 1967. *The Chinese in Cambodia.* Vancouver: University of British Columbia.

Wolf, E. 1982. *Europe and the People without History*. Berkeley: University of California Press.

Woll, Allen L., and Randall M. Miller. 1987. *Ethnic and Racial Images in American Film and Television: Historical Essays and Bibliography*. New York: Garland.

Wright, John C., and Aletha C. Huston. 1981. "Children's Understanding of the Forms of Television." In K. Hope, ed., *Viewing Children through Television*, pp. 73–88. London: Jossey-Bass.

Yanagisako, Sylvia J. 1987. "Mixed Metaphors: Nature and Anthropological Models of Gender and Kinship Domain." In Jane F. Collier and Sylvia J. Yanagisako, eds., *Gender and Kinship: Essays towards a Unified Analysis*, pp. 86–118. Palo Alto, Calif.: Stanford University Press.

Yao Sam Phon. 1988. *Chhŭap yŭm tôv aun* [Stop crying, my love]. Phnom Penh: Publications of the Cultural Foundation.

Yathay Pin. 1987. *Stay Alive My Son*. New York: Free Press.

Yeatman, G. W., et al. 1976. "Pseudobattering in Vietnamese Children." *Pediatrics* 58:616–17.

Yim Pisal. 1987. *Sântŭh sneh knŏng phloeng sângkream* [The bonds of love in the flames of war]. Paris: Cedoreck.

Yok Kun. 1984. *Chivĭt chheu chăp knŏng robâp Pŏl Pot, leng Sari* [The life of suffering during the Pol Pot, leng Sary period]. Phnom Penh: Publications of the Cultural Foundation.

———. 1986. *Thngai rĕah nôv Phoum thmey* [The sun rises over New Village]. Phnom Penh: Publications of the Cultural Foundation.

———. 1987. *Rong krŭah prŭah vongvéng* [Suffering from being lost]. Phnom Penh: Publications of the Cultural Foundation.

You Bo and B. Vuddh. 1986. *Krŏm kŏma khlôk tĭp* [The group of children of the magical gourd]. Phnom Penh: Publications of the Cultural Foundation.

Zborowski, Mark. 1952. Cultural Components in Response to Pain. *Journal of Social Issues* 8:16–30.

———. 1969. *People in Pain*. San Francisco: Jossey-Bass.

Zola, Irving. 1966. "Culture and Symptoms—An Analysis of Patients' Presenting Complaints." *American Sociological Review* 31:615–30.

Notes on Contributors

MAY M. EBIHARA is professor of anthropology at Lehman College and the Graduate Center, City University of New York. She is the only American anthropologist to have conducted ethnographic fieldwork in prewar Cambodia and is currently conducting research in the village in which she did her original research. She has written on Khmer kinship and social organization, religion, and women, among other subjects.

KAREN FISHER-NGUYEN did research with Khmer refugees in the Philippine Refugee Processing Center in 1986 and is completing a Ph.D. in linguistics from Cornell University.

MILADA KALAB studied at the universities of Prague, Santiniketan, Bombay, and London. She retired from her position as lecturer in the Department of Anthropology at the University of Durham in 1989. She did research in pre-1975 Cambodia and has more recently conducted research with refugees in Europe.

KHING HOC DY was born in Cambodia, where he taught Cambodian language and literature. He completed his Ph.D. in Cambodian literature in 1974 at the Université de Paris. He is senior research fellow at the Centre National de la Recherche Scientifique and a lecturer at the Institut national des Langues et Civilisations orientales in Paris.

Judy Ledgerwood received a doctorate in anthropology and Southeast Asian studies at Cornell University in 1990. She directed the Cornell University Library Book Conservation Project in Phnom Penh from October 1989 until 1991. She was a visiting professor of Asian Studies at Cornell University during the fall of 1991, and then conducted postdoctoral research in Cambodia, and taught anthropology at the University of Fine Arts in Phnom Penh. She is currently a Fellow of the Program for Cultural Studies at the East-West Center.

William Lobban is an Australian ethnomusicologist now teaching at the University of Fine Arts in Phnom Penh. He is also engaged in research in Khmer dance, music, and theater. He has an M.A. from the University of Hawaii in Pacific Islands Studies, having previously lived and worked in Melanesia and Western Polynesia.

John Marcucci received a Ph.D. in the Department of Anthropology at Southern Methodist University in 1986. He has conducted extensive research among Khmer refugees in the United States, with a focus on medical anthropology. He is currently Assistant Director of the Center for Highland Burma Peoples at the Institute for the Study of Earth and Man, Southern Methodist University.

John Marston is a graduate student in the Department of Anthropology at the University of Washington. He has degrees in English and English-as-a-Second Language and has worked as an English teacher and supervisor in Khao-I-Dang, a refugee camp in Thailand (1982), and the Refugee Processing Center in the Philippines (1985–86). He taught English in Cambodia during a stay in 1989 and has done research on Cambodians in the United States. He is currently in Cambodia conducting research.

Carol A. Mortland teaches anthropology at Dowling College. She has been a director of refugee programs on the local level and director of refugee services for a national voluntary agency. She received a doctorate in anthropology from the University of Oregon.

She has done research with Southeast Asian refugees since 1981 and has written on refugee patronage, refugee camp life, resettlement, and belief systems.

SAM-ANG SAM was born in Cambodia, where he studied music at the University of Fine Arts in Phnom Penh. He did graduate work at Connecticut College, received a Ph.D. in ethnomusicology from Wesleyan University, and was on the faculty at the University of Washington in Seattle. He is currently the director of the Cambodian Network Council in Washington, D.C. He is a well-known musician and ethnomusicologist who travels extensively presenting Khmer music to audiences throughout the world.

FRANK SMITH did graduate work in anthropology at Boston University in 1989–90. He has worked in various service capacities with refugees and co-coordinated the Cambodian language program at the Southeast Asian Studies Summer Institute in 1990 and again in 1993. Currently, he teaches and develops curriculum for bilingual ESL class for Cambodian adults in Boston. He has done extensive anthropological research with Khmer refugees in the United States.

Index